DRUNK ON ANGEL BREATH

R. NIKOLAS MACIOCI

R. Nikolas Macioci

Angel Breath: *A popular pink craft gin with an exquisitely fresh and playful fruity taste, directly infused with fragrant strawberries over several days.*

Copyright © 2024
Venetian Spider Press™ & R. Nikolas Macioci
All rights reserved.
ISBN: 979-8-9890481-8-2

Drunk on Angel Breath

With much love to my brother, Michael, who always stands beside me no matter what I'm standing in.

R. Nikolas Macioci

Foreword

Dr. R. Nikolas Macioci's poetry never disappoints. His work proves consistently worthwhile. His latest collection, *Drunk on Angel Breath*, is as evocative and savory as his dozens of previous award-winning works.

Macioci invites intrigue in the first line of "Interior Snow:" "It's snowing in the dining room tonight," while ironically, other lines are difficult to digest, due to how superbly they evoke heartache: "...The only place it's snowing is in my house/ but that's another story that almost kills/ me to tell. It's about a father who drank/ too much and raised welts on his kid..."

Macioci's collection attends to a variety of emotional palates. In "Euchre," he moves readers keenly into the speaker's experience: "...Bars are/ the game's prostitutes. They take tricks./ ...The only bar I understand is the one that serves beer/ and liquor, and I'm headed there now to help me/ forget everything I never learned about euchre."

The ease, vulnerability, and accessibility of each poem makes reading this collection very captivating. In "Uncle Bob," "The room is made of whispers." The poems' colors tantalize, locations simmer, and each character's triumph and wrinkled despair is written so deftly one can't devour each page fast enough. I highly recommend this most compelling masterpiece.

Sandra Feen
2022-2024 Ohio Beat Poet Laureate
Author of *Fragile Capacities: School Poems*,
Meat and Bone, *Evidence of Starving*, and
forthcoming: *There's a Rock on Martin Avenue*

R. Nikolas Macioci

Table of Contents

FOREWORD 5

PART ONE 11

    CANDY STOP 13
    BARTHMAN AVENUE CONFECTIONARY, 1949 15
    THE BOY WHO IDENTIFIED WITH FIREFLIES 17
    ONE OF THOSE WINTER EVENINGS 18
    ENTERING FEBRUARY AS A FIFTEEN-YEAR-OLD 19
    SPRING TRUANCY 21
    THE WALLET 23
    CANDLELIGHT 25
    ISLAND 27
    THREE MILES OUT OF LAURELVILLE, OHIO 31
    SHARED BRUISES 32
    IMPROVISATION ON A SUNNY DAY 34
    BIG WALNUT CREEK 36
    IN THE VACANT CATHEDRAL OF FRIDAY NIGHT 38
    THINGS THAT MATTER WHEN IT RAINS 39
    RITUAL DIVE 40
    INTERIOR SNOW 42
    ORNAMENTS 43
    SANCTUARY 44
    SMALL EXISTENCE 45
    ELEGY FOR A VIEWING 47
    OUTSIDE DENVER. COLORADO 48
    SEATTLE FATAL 50
    FIRST NIGHT IN SEATTLE, WASHINGTON 52
    RAIN STORY 54
    ONCE 55
    MEAT 57
    THE DRUNK 59
    INCIDENTAL SORROW 60
    UNTROUBLED BY DAD'S DEATH 62
    DRINKING BEER LATE AT NIGHT 63
    EVOCATION 64
    SURVIVOR'S WINDOW 66
    CANNING 68

PART TWO 69

    PREPARING FOR WINTER 71
    COLDNESS 72
    WINTERESQUE 73
    WINTER WALTZ 74
    AFTERWARD 75
    IRISES 76
    CREEPING PHLOX 77
    SUMMER DAY, 1913 78
    ODE TO OHIO CORNFIELDS 79
    SEPTEMBER INSTEAD OF LOVE 80
    AUTUMN AS LOVER 81
    THE INEXPRESSIBLE RAPTURE OF AN AUTUMN DAY 82
    TOWARD FALL 83
    OCTOBER FEELS LIKE A PLACE 84
    THE WORLD STUNNED BY LEAVES 85
    OCTOBER IS WHAT I AM 86
    AUTUMN WOMAN 87
    OF AUTUMN 88
    AUTUMN PARLORS 89
    A NOVEMBER LIFE 90
    ULTIMATE AUTUMN 91
    NEGOTIATING THE LAST DAY OF NOVEMBER 92
    PAINTING A NOVEMBER MOOD PIECE 93
    WHAT TO SAY AND FEEL IN AUTUMN 94
    AT THE FESTIVAL OF THE LEAVES 95

PART THREE 97

    THE RELUCTANT HUNTER 99
    UNCLE BOB 101
    THE ROUNDHOUSE 103
    GRANDPA MOHR 105
    A HALF DOZEN MIRRORS 107
    BLACK LAMB 108
    ALCHEMY FOR MOM 109
    SLEEPING MOTORCYCLES 111
    UNCLE HEINE'S WORLD 113
    ORIENT 115

PART FOUR 117

    DRUNK ON ANGEL BREATH 119

LIBRARY EPILOGUE 122
AMY LOWELL AND I 123
MY BEST EFFORT TO LEARN ABOUT DEATH 124
THE ICE ODOR OF BONE 125
THE ORGANIST 126
WHAT PEOPLE IN NEW YORK CITY KNOW ABOUT SUMMER 127
THIBAUDET PLAYS THE THIRD MOVEMENT FROM SAINT SAENS' PIANO CONCERTO NO. 5 129
THIS MAN, THIS SONG 130
A SIDELONG LOOK AT AN AGING WOMAN IN A CHAIR IN A NURSING HOME 132
BURN 133
DEATH CURE 135

PART FIVE **137**

THE SKIN ACT 139
WHAT HAPPENED AT THE CHATEAU 140
THE GIRL WHO PAID TO HAVE A MAN'S ARMS AROUND HER 141
SLEEPING WITH A NAZI 142
WEDDING AT THE HARTSTONE INN, CAMDEN, MAINE 143
UNCERTAIN TENDERNESS 145
THE APPRENTICE'S SELF-PORTRAIT 146
THE EASE WITH WHICH YOU DEAL WITH DANGEROUS BOYS 148
THERE HAS NEVER BEEN A MORE SUCCESSFUL WOMAN 150
UNBEARABLE AND FIERCE MERCY 151
THE NOTHING THAT GROWS INSIDE OF ME 153
LOVE IN A FIELD OF POPPIES 154
SAKURA 155
  The Japanese word for cherry blossoms *155*
THINGS I'LL NEVER TOUCH AGAIN 156
CAREFUL RETURN 157
SINGING THE SONG OF WANTING SOMETHING OUT OF REACH 159

PART SIX **161**

GOURMET HOSPITAL FOOD 163
EUCHRE 164
BATTLE FOR NAPKINS 166
A GOOD MYSTERY NEVER KILLED ANY BODY 168
THE DOUBLE EDGE OF OWNING A PARROT 169
IF BIRDS WERE MONEY 170
WASHINGTON CIRCLE 171
THREE HOURS FROM ATHENS, GREECE, 1970 173
PHANTASMAGORIC MIGRATION 175

ESCAPADE	176
GAS STATION BLUES	178
ZOOMING	180
TIME ON THE MOON	181
ASSET FROM ANOTHER WORLD	182
PART SEVEN	**185**
NO WORDS	187
SKY'S WHORE	189
THE POET WANTS MORE THAN POETRY	190
MORE UPBEAT POEMS PLEASE	192
ABOUT THE AUTHOR	**193**

PART ONE

> "My memoir is a story of family and childhood, and everyone has had one of those. Mine is not the definitive version of childhood, but it's a great way to start a conversation."
>
> Sue Perkins

> "I think many people need, even require, a narrative version of their life. I seem to be one of them. Writing memoir is, in some ways, a work of wholeness."
>
> Sue Monk Kidd

R. Nikolas Macioci

CANDY STOP

I met my nemesis when I was six,
in the first grade at Reeb Avenue
Elementary School. Recess lasted an hour,
time enough for students to go home
for lunch and stop on the way back
at one of two confectionaries.

On this particular day, returning to school,
I stopped at Bellman's. I leaned over
the glass-top counter and asked for twenty-five
cents worth of penny candy. The clerk sacked
my purchase into a brown, paper bag.
I clutched the bag, traipsed three blocks
to the schoolyard and waited for the bell to ring.

Brent Thompson, the school's bully, slouched
toward me, asked for a piece of candy.
I handed him a Mary Jane. He unwrapped it,
dropped the paper on the ground, and stuffed
the candy into his fat jaw. One piece wasn't enough
to satisfy him, so he snatched the bag
from my hand. Contrary to my parents' advice
not to fight, I punched him in the face. The teacher
on duty raced to separate us. She paraded
Brent and me to the principal's office.

Mr. Callahan's work space dwelled like an evil eye
watching us ascend twelve wooden steps
from the main floor. I climbed each tread,
fearful of the consequence. Even though
I explained what had happened, Mr. Callahan decided
we warranted a paddling. I bent over first.
The good point was the paddle didn't have holes.
Nevertheless, my butt burned like the proverbial bush
in the Bible.

When I slumped home, my parents, notified
about the incident, sent me to my room.
 I looked out the bedroom window at leaves falling
from a pin oak tree, thought about how I had fallen
from my parents' grace because of a bag of penny candy
and the grasping grab of a bonafide bully.

Drunk on Angel Breath

BARTHMAN AVENUE CONFECTIONARY, 1949

Mom unties her apron after hours
of dipping ice cream and filling Coke glasses.
She leaves the store, climbs steel stairs
on the outside of the stucco building
to our upstairs apartment, her weariness
clear as water. Faint crow's feet show
at the corners of her thirty-seven-year-old eyes.

Because my parents work long hours in the store,
I have no particular place to go. I roam
the neighborhood, scout alleys for treasure
in trash barrels. I'm eight, out of school
for the summer, have permission to go barefoot.
Sidewalks, however, scald, require sandals.

With my cloth bag of marbles and wearing
a homemade Durango Kid outfit,
I round up friends to play cowboys on dirt paths
behind the building. A game of marbles follows.

Now and then, I enter the store, loiter
on a soda-fountain stool, see the same lady
buy paperback books every time I'm there.
Urchins in dirty shorts, barely old enough to walk,
flop nickels onto the glass case for penny candy.
I think there are a few wealthy families at this end
of town, but most South Enders, my parents tell me,
are poor. That is why it seems to me
much of the world wears rags. Once a month,
after closing time, to keep dust down,
Dad oils floorboards.

Earlier in the day, in short pants, toting a pup tent,
I searched for a green yard among all the concrete,
ended up draping canvas over stacks of beer cases
in the store's back room. Now, I wait for Dad to finish
mopping and for Mom to clean counters. Tired
of gazing at a neon Burger Beer sign, I decide to go
upstairs ahead of them. I push open the fly-specked
screen door, step down onto July's residual heat
that still emanates from the sidewalk
like a leftover remnant of summer.

THE BOY WHO IDENTIFIED WITH FIREFLIES

They pepper the dark with miniature, gold
torches. I am nine years old and have nothing
to do but carry a Mason jar into the backyard,
unscrew the top, and use the bottom to catch
these docile bugs. They are night's yellow
beacons, easy to grab from blue-black sky.

I have caught a dozen or so in my jar.
They make no sound, and it doesn't disturb
them when I flick my finger against the glass.
I call them *lightning bugs*, but the book says
they are fireflies. They blink like amber eyes.
I've seen some kids tear off the abdomen
and wear it on their finger like a ring. I cannot
be so cruel. Soon I will turn them loose, but
for a while longer I want to look at their flashing
beams, captured bits and pieces of sun.

I've ended with a pretty good catch. Now,
it's time to open the lid and let them go.
I recap the jar. My dad yells from the porch.
I slump toward the steps, wonder why
someone doesn't free me from his mean streak
that keeps the lid screwed tight
on a jar that suffocates what is captured.

R. Nikolas Macioci

ONE OF THOSE WINTER EVENINGS

Equipped with scissors, I head toward the shed,
a plywood structure with spaces
between the boards. Mom has handed me over
to her friend, Ann, while she celebrates her
divorce and vacations for two weeks in Florida.
To secure a touch of home, I have brought a
box full of clippings, but the real treasure lies
in the shed among stacks of old newspapers.
I am a ninety-one pound twelve year old who
lives inside his own world and cuts posters from
movie magazines. The lure of the shed is
an opportunity to add to my clippings.

With my head down, I hurry through a February
snow squall to the shed door. I have been given
a key and permission to rummage through the old
newspapers, my objective: to make a surrogate
family from comic strips.

I choose Gasoline Alley and Brenda Starr,
look through voluminous stacks for those
comics. If I find enough for a storyline,
I can step into an imagined world where
abusive dads, divorce and hurt do not exist.
My hand aches from gripping scissors
for over an hour in the cold. By the time
I stop cutting, daylight has dimmed to twilight.

That night, I lie in bed with my box of clippings.
Lamplight catches snow blowing across the
window, and I am satisfied and content to belong
to the untroubled existence of paper lives.

ENTERING FEBRUARY AS A FIFTEEN-YEAR-OLD

I shivered, cold, numb from skating
too long on the pond in Welches' Woods.
Skates slung over a shoulder, I trudged steps
from the woods into an adjoining cornfield
where moonlight filled stubble and spread
a white sheen. I drew down in my coat,
but despite its warmth, the glacial bite
of winter penetrated my Mackinaw.

I lived across the road at the end
of the field, and though I had only
a hundred feet to go, icy wind picked up,
and it began to snow. A million flakes
flickered past me, dappled my face
like cold kisses.

I reached the drainage ditch along the road,
crossed over to the front yard of my house.
A lamp in the window sent forth yellow light
like a welcoming context of safety.
I could barely fathom that I had arrived.

Inside, after warming up, I gazed
through the picture window at snow beginning
to stick to utility poles, accumulate
on cypress bushes in the terrace, the world
outside disappearing by the minute.
For some reason, I remembered this morning's
shaving cut when being alive seemed less
habit than surprise, and I stopped shaving
to let my mind touch on how quick the absence
of life occurs.

I snapped on the porchlight, night, dark
as an African Black Beetle, brightened
a path with a handful of illumination.
I stood still listening, idle as lawlessness,
for the first time consciously realizing
snow has no sound. Outside was quiet
as my stepdad's parked Ford. My parents
had gone to a bingo game in the Mercury.
I lit another lamp, felt listless and alone.
For the moment, I lived in an empty house,
lighting lamps to burn away solitude.

SPRING TRUANCY

Woods loom across the field from my house
on Moler Road. I enter dense thicket, hear
a woodpecker hammer a resistant tree.
Although leaves have started to unfurl,
daffodils bloom, this third week in March
remains unpredictable and cold.
I wear a fur-collared, waist-length jacket,
carry school books for my senior classes.
I've missed the bus deliberately, planned
absence from school and a sojourn
into the woods several days ago.

I find the bridle path of the riding academy
that abuts the woods. The path oozes mud
from winter thaw. I step from grassy patch
to grassy patch on my way to the pond
in the middle of the acreage. I arrive
at the clearing. Wind ripples the pond's water.
A fallen tree trunk, near water's edge,
looks like a perfect place to stretch out
for a nap. It's still early in the morning,
dewy. I lie down on the log, let sun warm me.

I have to stay here until school is out
and the bus passes my house. Then,
I can start home. I'm the first and last passenger
on the route. Above me, a swallow sails low
looking for insects. I close my eyes, doze.

R. Nikolas Macioci

The next time I open them, my Timex reads
one o' clock. School dismisses at 3:15.
I open my literature book, continue to memorize
Frost's "Spring Pools." It's not a school assignment,
but a choice I made because I like the poet's work,
and it's a poem appropriate to recite when I'm here.

I start back toward the field, wait at the edge of trees
for the school bus to pass, which it does, empty
of everyone, including me.

THE WALLET

Billy, the next-door bully on Moler Road,
waits at the rusted, chain-link fence
for my six-year-old brother, Michael, to come out
and play. Pudgy Billy weighs more
than my brother, likes to pin Michael
to the ground when they wrestle. In short,
he simply wants to antagonize.

Mom is not the neighboring type, keeps
her distance. On the other hand,
Billy's grandmother, May, likes to catch Mom
at the fence and gossip. May is a good person,
but quirky.

In 1959, when I graduated
from Marion Franklin High School,
May bought me a brown wallet. She didn't know
I don't carry any because when I take one out
of my pocket, I usually leave it behind. I did,
however, slide photos of school friends
into its plastic frames. I also slipped my draft card
and Social Security card into the billfold.
For over sixty years, it has lain
in my top, bureau drawer. I see its deteriorating
leather every time I open the drawer.

May and Mom are dead now, our house demolished,
property a paved parking lot for school buses.
Most of the people whose pictures are in my wallet
have died, too. I ask myself why I keep it?
I think it has something to do with death and time.
It's a piece of surviving evidence that there was a 1959,
a mom, a May, a rusty fence that, as Robert Frost wrote,
makes good neighbors.

CANDLELIGHT

Each of us held a candle. Its light streaked
our faces as we lit the wick of the person
to our right. A chorus of voices led us
in Gloria in excelsis Deo. Doors were closed
against a foot of Christmas Eve snow.

I was nineteen and rapt by the religious
ceremony. For that moment, I suspended
disbelief, felt sure of the truth of God.
Was it the music, the candlelight, worshiping
as a group that opposed agnosticism?
I was not a member of the church.
I was a one-event guest who wanted
to experience a candlelight service.

I became a little dizzy from the uptake
of emotion. If I had looked in a mirror,
I would have seen a flushed face.
The spell lasted a few more seconds
before the minister asked us to extinguish
our candles.

My spiritual self broke into pieces.
I had been mesmerized by decorum
and ritual, invited to a gathering
to celebrate Christ. In other words,
like Amahl, I had been a night visitor
who had sung his heart out to believe.

ISLAND

The cabin cruiser sputters to a stop
along the wooden dock. Dute, my cousin,
springs from his vessel, ties the dock line
to a cleat. A low, gray sky hangs over
McGregor Bay, Canada as Aunt Clara, wearing
a flowered housedress and a diamond necklace
with stones as big as thumbnails, strides down
boardwalk to greet two of her sisters, my
mom, stepdad, my brother, Mike, and me.
Behind her, a three-story, white house
with green trim looms like a citadel atop rock.
Aunt Clara and Uncle Forest purchased
the Island, which included the house, in 1939.
They called the island "Camp." Uncle Forest's
story had become family legend.

He quit school after third grade. Because
of having a fiery temperament, he couldn't work
for anyone. Self-employment became inevitable.
While a young adult, he borrowed money
to buy his first piece of machinery,
placed it in the basement of the half-double
he and his wife rented, and produced his first
airplane part. Wealth became his badge,
and he wore it with quiet arrogance
and cold satisfaction.

During supper, and sputtering gossip
about other millionaires in the bay,
Aunt Clara announces that she has accepted,
in advance of our arrival, an invitation
for my brother and me to attend
a young people's party on a neighboring island.

Dute's wife, Rita, familiar with navigating
the bay and thereabouts, drives the boat,
points out shoals, scares us with comments
regarding the unmeasurable water over which
we speed.

A boy about seventeen meets us at the dock.
Like Aunt Clara's, the island consists
of rock and pine. Even in blue shadows
of twilight, I discern specific signs of wealth:

seven guest houses, a tennis court,
and several boats. We follow the boy
up wooden walkway to a mansion-like lodge,
half wood, half glass. Inside, warmth flares
from a granite fireplace. Beamed ceiling
in the great room, slate floor, leather sofa
and chairs, plus original art broadcast
expensive taste, conspicuous as a bumper
sticker. I deem it a place where all needs
are granted.

Drunk on Angel Breath

A slim girl with perfect teeth stubs out
a cigarette, offers me drink choices,
hands me a bottle of beer I've never heard of,
and a glass I assume to be Waterford.
A young man with green eyes, brown hair,
and a medium-strong handshake, flops
down beside me. I know in an instant
his popularity commands the room.
Colton knows how to focus attention
on the other person, and I feel comfortable
answering innocuous questions. His eyes
turn toward the fireplace where a boy
called Alex pulls a chair near the hearth.
Alex, with long, braided, black hair
and bone-white skin, strums a guitar
and sings folk songs. A girl, opposite him,
leans forward, intent on either him or
his music. He smiles at her, and I believe
seconds of lust surface between them,
and I wonder if they need music to want
one another?

Music ends. Colton slips to the fireplace,
kneels, as if to be tapped for knighthood,
lays a couple logs on the grate, pokes flames
from pinkish ash, returns to lounge beside me.

By now, all nine of us are inebriated, relaxed
as flat tires. Colton asks if I've read Fromm's
The Art of Loving. I answer yes, and know
our conversation has become philosophical
and personal. He says that an old man
in a room can be worth as much as a couple,
wags a hand in the direction of the two
near the fireplace. I feel an electric moment
between us.

I rise to leave. A blade of lightning jumps
off sky. Walls of rain occlude sight as we
wend our way to the boat. Colton follows
to see us off. The boy who tended the fire
pats me on the shoulder, says he's glad
we met. I say likewise, and know then
his charm will invade my dreams,
luminous as the intimacy of rain.

Drunk on Angel Breath

THREE MILES OUT OF LAURELVILLE, OHIO

I'm hiking along a dirt road on Saddle Hill,
stop for a moment to hear a crow on a fence,
wonder if the crow's bones are light enough
for the bird to fly off the earth. Standing still,
I wait for movement in the underbrush,
for a brown-faced chipmunk or a rattlesnake,
gray as limestone, fangs sharp as the edge
of a tin can lid, to surface in a swatch of sunlight.
A red-tailed hawk swoops over my head.
When I look up, sky burns a yellow glare.
In an adjacent field, I spot coneflowers, clover,
can smell pungent, livestock odors. I amble on,
think how nothing lasts. Even death dies.
For some reason I remember Salvatore Dali's
draped clocks, wish I could paint a picture
of clocks in the wind, coming apart
with noiseless crashes. I shake my thoughts
away from surrealism, trudge onward in July heat.

In another field, a draft horse's tail swats flies
from its rear, shakes its head until the mane blurs.
I stop to watch, detect no sign of death
in the patient neck, polished skin, and yet death
will someday demand this horse. I look because
there's nothing else to do when the horse and I
are fenced in by time. Nearby, on a post,
a blue-winged warbler chirps. Its joy, I think,
as I start down the road to finish my trek,
counts for little against providence
and the omnipresent shadow of demise.

SHARED BRUISES

We held similar affection for *Winesburg, Ohio*
sophomore winter at The Ohio State University,
became immediate friends in American Literature.
Both of us had shelved *War and Peace*, didn't think
Napoleonic Wars compelling as small-town life.

We lingered near windows tinted smoke,
wind dropping an unkind zero in Denny Hall's
vacant conference room.

We disappeared into shadows of ourselves,
two voices astonished by Sherwood Anderson's accuracy
in depicting our own isolation. We watched embellishments
of snow, trees wearing polar-bear coats.
From my breast pocket, I wriggled out my written poem,
handed it to her. Angling for light, she read. I waited.
She said I described loneliness as a truth without cure,
absent embrace. We had seen sadness
in each other, dangling in our hearts
like a loose button we thought literature could mend.
Maybe that was attraction.

Drunk on Angel Breath

After graduation, thirty years passed without
physical contact. I received a teaching award,
was asked to speak in a Hilton hotel.
I found her in the audience.
We exchanged amenities; shallowness updated us.
I searched for that old, habitual anguish.
She dominated my time beyond courtesy, while others
waited to congratulate. She was no longer
that winter day person from memory, or the diffident
girl who sent postcards from Florence, wrote romantic
reactions about major landmarks. I faced someone
less sensitive, a bit hardened.

When she turned to leave, I couldn't help thinking
she supplanted melancholy with thick skin, stitched
it in place with callousness, cold indifference.
I watched her disappear up an aisle,
felt nothing but regret.

R. Nikolas Macioci

IMPROVISATION ON A SUNNY DAY

I believe in silence of sun. Noiseless
light falls across my body. I shut eyes,
listen to the sound of breath, calm, barely
audible. The room fills with solar warmth.
For the moment, I care about nothing but
the monotonous ticking of the clock. I hold
my hand out, study wrinkled fingertips, dare
to think life is without end.

Wrapped in peace of this windless
December day, I defy death to point its finger
while I sit in my chair, collect sunlight
as if it were a guarantee of immortality.

This is how I fight depression
and other animals of the mind such as
the nameless creature that keeps opening
a door on loneliness.

So far, what do I have to show for today,
a little bit of lolling in sunlight?
I will lose even that once the room overflows
with night. Neither light nor darkness
fills empty hands. Whatever plan providence
has for me, love is not part of it.

Drunk on Angel Breath

Sometime after birth, I simply picked up
the wrong script, have always had to improvise
rare moments of happiness. I have accumulated
years of hunger to be touched. It started when
I was seven years old, wondered what I had done
so bad that Dad beat me instead of holding me
in his arms. To mend my heart, I turned
to movies, clipped poster ads, kept them
in a box that I carried almost everywhere.

Clouded now, the sun, a yellow bruise on the sky,
has drifted behind a cedar tree. The earth and I
keep moving toward total absence of light.

BIG WALNUT CREEK

Whenever I cross a bridge over a creek,
I want to pull to the berm and slide out.
Something mysterious draws me to a creek
the way meditation moves me toward peace.

Tree branches overhang either side
of brown water, create a cave effect,
a refuge from random racket.

Fishermen's paths lead to the water,
ground hardened from frequent use.
I wonder who else walks these paths
of shadowy sun, twisted tree trunks?
A loner? Someone like myself
with a ready camera?

When I was young, I swam in deep sections
of Big Walnut Creek, fished where eddies swirled
around fallen trees.

Now, in September, ash trees have turned
cat's eye yellow. Red oak leaves burn
against a forget-me-not blue sky.
I park along Alum Creek. On the path, I pass
beneath apricot color of black gum trees,
linger under a bridge, listen to traffic
speed over my head, vibrate pylons.

Drunk on Angel Breath

I snap numerous pictures, try different
perspectives, pause to listen to cicadas'
sound like small, stuttering engines.

Light grows less, and I climb the bank
to my car, the trail becoming black
as licorice.

R. Nikolas Macioci

IN THE VACANT CATHEDRAL OF FRIDAY NIGHT

It's Friday, and I'm staring at black
night on the other side of the window.
If I shift my focus, I can barely see
an image of myself through which the
lights on Main Street shine. It's clever
how invisibility works with just a shift
of eye focus.

During Friday nights, I wait
for the possible. My whole life
has been marking time for the beginning
of something with another person.
When I think of waiting, I think
of Penelope who, while she stood by
ten years for Odysseus' return,
used her own shadow for companionship.
Odysseus did return, embraced her,
caressed her cheek. I want that
kind of romance, someone to teach me
how to reach for sunshine on a dark day,
someone stripping me of doubt, becoming
the best friend I ever had.

THINGS THAT MATTER WHEN IT RAINS

I once loved to be in the rain, but age
and decorum stole impetuosity.
Now, when it rains, I sprawl on a lawn chair
on the front porch, listen to rhythmic
repetition, hoping there isn't a hole in the roof.
I don't doze. I dissolve into a kind of sadness,
wait for a phone call from no one in particular.
I stare at apartments down the street, wonder
how many people in them are drinking
themselves into oblivion tonight, victims
of unfulfillment in the dark hallways
in which they live and love.

When it rains, I look for closeness
with someone. It's not a simple thing to want.
It's as complicated as a cat's cradle.
From the corner of my eye I spot a police car
cruising down my one-way road where
we've never had an incident. Even though
he's trained to look for trouble, maybe
he just wants to be where there is none.
His windshield wipers clear the glass
at top speed. He turns around, leaves.
Silver hammers of rain continue to pound
the road, and I continue to watch for another
human to make a turn in my direction.

RITUAL DIVE

Ever since I'd dreamed of doing so,
to dive into Indian Lake at night
felt necessary. For a weekend getaway,
I'd rented a ninety-five-dollar-a day
cabin within walking distance of water.
The lake shimmered a hint of blue under
golden glare of sunlight, and I'd swum
through such sunlight yesterday afternoon
when I arrived. The dream, however,
had awakened me to a compulsive urge
to risk a night dive. Though only
eighty-five miles from where I live
in Groveport, Ohio, Indian Lake felt
like an exotic escape, and the idea
of entering foreign water at night
seemed irresistibly adventurous.

Whereas sun sparkled water in daylight,
tonight, moon, the size and color
of a white, overcoat button, casts
a milky path to the dock on which
I ready myself for the dive.

Drunk on Angel Breath

My curved body falls forward through
moon's watery skin that heals shut
behind me. In an instant, I turn
into a comic book hero, wear a liquid
cape that lets me surface like a surprise.
I dog paddle in place, hold my head
as high as I can, loose, neck skin stretches
tight as a young man's. Legs kick aside
resistance, body slices through water,
a living knife. Arms steer to the ladder.
I pull myself up. Pearls of moonlight
roll off me. Content, like after a baptism,
I'm satisfied to have taken handsful of night
with me as if I were on a spiritual journey
with a sacred purpose.

R. Nikolas Macioci

INTERIOR SNOW

It's snowing in the dining room tonight,
piling up to the seat of my chair. For hours,
I have shoveled and carried bucketfuls
of crystalline flakes outside. After all,
it is December in my house, and a person
can expect snow to drift from anywhere.
Tornadic spirals rise up when I open the door.
Dusting off my chair, I sit near a window
for a while. Stars blink their meager light.
The only place it's snowing is in my house,
but that's another story that almost kills
me to tell. It's about a father who drank
too much and raised welts on his kid,
a father who, when sober, killed
everyone near him with clever kindness.

I've shoveled down to the hardwood floor,
carried out the last bucket, although,
a light snow continues to fall. Outside,
Christmas lights baptize the night,
snowflakes melt atop the stove lit
with burners high. The funny thing is,
there are no holes in the ceiling.
Winter simply drifts down the way
ghosts enter through the wall.
Cold has become a religion.
Look at my blue hands, fingers nearly
frozen, wanting only warmth
of my father's hand in mine.

ORNAMENTS

Company gone, the house seems blessed
with silence. I flop into a wingback chair,
focus on the Christmas tree. I squint eyes
for effect, and bulbs look like scribbled electric.
Paper angels peppered with glitter twist
from register heat. If I screw up my eyes
and move my head, decorations look like
a blur of buried treasure.

I lounge for a while longer, sip Merlot.
Memory retrieves times when family
occupied these pieces of furniture,
their laughter diluted with Budweiser,
veins overflowing with warmth, unlimited time.

I snap the porch light on, gaze
at snow-covered lawn, summon them from graves.
They shrug off death's chill, enter the house,
bend into favorite places, form a familiar tableau.
In stunning stillness, I hear their voices offer
a thousand good wishes, and then I'm back
to myself, look at my reflection in a glass bauble,
accept limits of the real world.

SANCTUARY

I have learned how to leave the earth
in a wise way. I trust dreams to take me
beyond sleep, to a safe place where
I can accept sadness.

Asleep, I saw smooth faces
of my younger parents and
soda-fountain-security
a nine year old had
when his mom and dad owned
the confectionery on Barthman Avenue.
In that sleep, loss appeared less
extraordinary, less likely to haunt.

Outside, a loose shutter bangs
against November gales. The furnace
clicks on, and a stream of warmth rolls
across carpet. Snow is forecast.
Dark clouds validate the prediction.
I grab a quilt, cover myself for a nap,
anticipate, through unprotected memory
of middle age, that good dreams will speak
to me again in my sleeping ear.

SMALL EXISTENCE

I needed a haircut the day I ambled
past watered lawns and open windows
to Forest Cemetery three miles out
of Circleville, Ohio. Maple leaves,
spinach green, shaded black, wrought-iron
gates streaked with pigeon droppings.
May light stretched white glare across
acres of tombstones.

For hours, I searched granite dates
to find the oldest, dawdled
over manicured sod, thinking graves
were beautiful but worthless.

Over a rise at the back of the cemetery,
Scioto River glittered between shores,
late afternoon sun flashing last brilliance
off water. If I squinted, the river looked
like a sea. I folded down cross-legged
on the bank. Shadows had begun to fringe
the cemetery. I stared at the river, and
a great calm centered in my chest.
For the moment, I didn't look behind me
at patches of earth where a thousand bodies
lay lost to an exasperating but precise silence.
As an affirmation of being alive,
I scattered some stones into the water.
When I rose to start back, bird noises
and leaf movement had stopped.

On my way to the gate, I passed the mausoleum,
thought many people believe it to be a place
to inter a body for a guarantee of everlasting life.

Because I had lingered too long, I deserved
the caretaker's suspicious watchfulness.
He unchained the gate, and I left.

Across the street, a knot of kids wedged close
to the inside window of a Dairy Queen. I ordered
a chocolate cone, perched at a wooden picnic table,
watched night remove the cemetery stone by stone,
mouth full of ice cream and alibis against immortality.

ELEGY FOR A VIEWING

You use everything you ever learned
about good behavior, approach the door,
open it on cut flowers that smell like death.
You fall in line with other people's sorrow,
adjust eyesight dimmed by glare of afternoon.
Most here have reached the age when a
death strips them of pretense. At the casket,
you gaze drowsily, not exactly sure what
you are supposed to see. Makeup that
inexpertly imitates sleep catches your eye
first. Then the hands become your focus.
Were they always as wrinkled as wadded-up
gloves? In minutes, you are finished giving
attention to the corpse, and someone else
wiggles close to you to take a turn.

The room becomes congested, and more
folding chairs appear as if by magic.
"Sign the book. Don't forget to sign the book,"
someone says to another person behind you.
You jot your signature, turn to leave.
Amiable hands shake yours, thank you
for coming.

You step outside, grateful to be away
from the promise of eternity, happy
for bright blue sky, consoled by light
as if you had just invented the sun.

OUTSIDE DENVER. COLORADO

Like morning communion, ground clouds
evaporates on a tongue of sun. We have pulled
to the berm to snap photos of Pikes Peak.
My three travel-mates open car doors, slam them
shut. Metal echoes follow these companions
as they wade through bluebells, Indian paintbrush,
and thistle. They press cameras to their eyes,
ready, eager to bring home souvenir shots
of the Rockies.

I take pleasure in being alone for the moment.
From the dashboard stereo, Kenny G's saxophone
sweetens the air with "Songbird." My friends
have trudged deeper into the field, look like
lost errants who have wondered off course.
Sun through glass, a cosmic arm around my
solitude, warms away a forenoon chill.

Drunk on Angel Breath

I think I could hide here forever, throw away
my name, become as content as the Lark Bunting
settled on the post of a piece of abandoned fence.
When friends return and open car doors, tranquility
flies elsewhere like seeds from a milkweed pod.

Back home, in a freezing moment of winter,
I will remember welcome isolation beside this road,
gigantic mountains yellowed by early morning
sun, serenity at my fingertips, and, yes, I will retrieve
my own photos from the trip, preserve the best one
in a frame from Walmart, place it near lamplight
on a desk where no songbird will be singing.

R. Nikolas Macioci

SEATTLE FATAL

I'm not rich, but I have enough money
and loose change in my pocket to fly
to Seattle for a week's vacation and afford
a fifty-five-dollar-a-night hotel room
in a disreputable part of town.
Before going out to explore the district,
I raise a window in lieu of an air conditioner
that dangles like defeat on the window's edge
and won't turn on. A strip of white curtain,
turned gray as abandoned wedding veils, hangs
on either side. Pink and orange swirls
of cloud initiate sunset, a backdrop
for unsavory behavior below. Headlights
reveal pimps, prostitutes, and weary travelers
who watch from the sidelines. I don a blue
golf shirt and khaki shorts. The August night
is as hot as a day in Death Valley.

I leave the room, step into the hallway
onto worn, red, flowered carpet. Stale cigarette
odor permeates the air. I wait beside bronze
elevator doors. In the elevator, a man
and woman watch me with brief glances.

Drunk on Angel Breath

Outside, under half-burnt-out light from
the hotel's neon sign, a red-hot tongue
offering dark a promiscuous kiss, I linger,
count upward to locate my room on the fifth
floor. Some windows are squares of yellow
illumination, rectangles of butter on red brick.
I find my room, wonder how many people
have lain on the single bed, smoking a cigarette,
the last-stop room that looks the same anywhere
in the world.

I amble on down Aurora Avenue North,
most corners occupied by shadowy figures,
offers of sex, stories of unfulfillment.
Two men slump against a building's wall,
share a bottle in a paper bag, argue unintelligible sounds.

In six more days, I will board the plane to Columbus, Ohio.
Cornfields will shine a green innocence below,
and I will be wiser from the teachings of night,
from the many, disaffected lives that settle for the street.

R. Nikolas Macioci

FIRST NIGHT IN SEATTLE, WASHINGTON

I want you, your skyscrapers that hoard space
like misers of heaven, your old, young homeless
who believe they are closer to death
than the rest of us. I want your shops
full of bed sheets and shoe displays. I want
hat-wearing-women whose faces have been
arranged by Elizabeth Arden and who hope
their high heels will put them above ordinary
women. I want the well-built men
whose sheepish eyes regard everything
and who seem to see everything
as if they see nothing, who will kill
and who never seem to die themselves.
I want the continuous traffic that surrounds
like a bad dream and the evening neon
on an electric leash. I want the pimps
and the prostitutes who sell a moment of flesh.

Drunk on Angel Breath

I want to stop at each corner to assess
if I have outwalked the feverish urge
to pick a joint in this disreputable West End
and have a beer while I wait for someone
to step from smokey semi-dark and care
to sit behind me. I want to remember
there will be no embrace for anyone
but the young and the fortunate. I want
to dawdle down Pike Street, maybe
find myself munching on a sandwich in a
back-alley diner. I want the hungry gulls
blown into Puget Sound on random currents.
I want the satisfaction of being able
to take this city for granted, unable to hear
the bark of a starving dog on a chain in a city
this size, and I want the fulfillment
of taking down the sky each night
by simply closing the hotel's curtains.

RAIN STORY

I drive home in the rain, thinking
I have empty hands and sleep alone.
Even as streets become lakes,
I would stop and talk to a stranger.
Outside, people are turning into water
as I confess that I would welcome
almost anyone into my house,
a head on a pillow next to mine.

At home, in the foyer, I glance at a mirror,
see loneliness, desperation, the hated sight
of such sadness. Look what rain has done to me.
It wallops windows, makes me wish
the worst people in my life were back in it again.
I would prefer to laugh about despair, but
that moment is buried in the impotence I feel
about my own fate.

The rain is slowing down to a drizzle.
I don't hear it anymore. It has made
transparent jewels on the window.
I wait for the whisper in my ear
from someone else. This is how
the sky gave me rain, and the rain ruined me.

Drunk on Angel Breath

ONCE

I may never see my wife or the boy again.
I'm fifty years old, once thought love
hovered inside me for a family
who let me down. I admit I pushed them
like firewood from one year to another
right down into the flames of my drunkenness.

I once flew down streets shaking a gun
at God, brain dark from drink, spitting air
behind their heads with raging curses.
They hid from me in relatives' houses,
disappeared into safer environments,
into each other like a two-petaled flower.
I kicked aside trash cans in Southend alleys,
skinned knees sliding upon gravel
as I searched for their whereabouts.
Eventually, I sought home, collapsed
upon the couch, uncomfortable
with woozy thoughts about their absence.

Next morning, they stole through the door,
silent as thieves. My head ached and I felt
breakable. I showered, ready to dignify
my wrongs at the dinner table. I had traded
them for the blanked-out world of drink.

R. Nikolas Macioci

We sat down together, and I gazed
at the wife who couldn't seize my arm
to protect herself and at the son who seemed
to be sweating great clouds of dread.
Their eyes appeared thankful for civil moments,
but I pushed away from the table,
fumbled a bottle of beer from refrigerator's
bright coldness and shuffled toward the living room
and the impending shock of divorce.

MEAT

The Sunday afternoon I refused to eat meat,
Mom had gone to work in the confectionary
below the apartment in which we lived
on Barthman Avenue. My father's tyrannical
shadow loomed behind my seven-year-old
back as I stared at the slice of pot roast.
He insisted I eat the meat. I hated meat,
but had managed in the past to swallow
a few bites with Mom in the wings urging me
to eat more.

My gag reflex anticipated
the first mouthful. Surrendering to his threats,
I pulled a strip from a large chunk, gagged
at the tear of fiber, the separation of brown,
ribbon-like strings. I forced the forkful
into the darkness of my nausea.
He wasn't satisfied with pretense
of eating, and struck me. His slap burned.
I focused on cabinets, intent on dark
grain, thought about dishes safe behind closed
doors. I felt tightness around my upper torso.
Before I could realize his next move,
he wound rope around my waist and chest.
His anger improvised a gag from a dish towel.
I shrank away from hope that Mom would enter
and take my side against the undershirted dad
who warned me to bestow thanks for my food.

R. Nikolas Macioci

Tonight, I write this poem about escape.
I see it once more, eventual release
from ropes, the blast of breath into my lungs
when he finally removed the gag.
My forehead ached. Eventually, I swallowed
the meat, my last vision of that dinner:
asking to be excused from the table.

THE DRUNK

He rolls naked to a sitting position,
mumbles about forgetting, points
a gun of disregard at me, belt replete
with usual bullets of inattention.
The movie he promised
begins in less than three hours.
My twelve-year-old mind knows
routine: We will catch a bus downtown,
stop, at least once, at a beer joint.

He wobbles to his feet, dresses, asks
how Mom is. Their divorce final,
Mom and I prize freedom from his cruelty.

Four months in bed with rheumatic fever,
I watched daylight brighten windows,
nighttime with dark.
I worried he, drunk, would whip me
out of bed as thoughtlessly as he might
snap a sapling from a woods.

In the theater, he slumps into a seat,
head lolls, face slackens
to a stream of snores. I fidget, disgusted
that he has slid away to oblivion, stare
at the screen without seeing the movie,
ache for the dad I have not yet acquired.

R. Nikolas Macioci

INCIDENTAL SORROW

My dad finally died today after false starts,
finished for real, unlike his frequent, fabricated
lies about his own death that often followed
Mom and me into hiding. Eyes stuffed with fear,
we would huddle together, try to fold
into ourselves and disappear, but
he always thrust back into our lives, bloodshot
eyes blistering our faces with fear.
Today, his drooping, muscular neck is dead,
and Mom and I wear survival like corsages
of self-congratulation.

Ghost faces of his shenanigans drift
through my mind again like bad clouds,
chill me like December's sad icicles.
Now, we own white truth of relief,
and can safely reminisce about the red-haired
hooker who ripped him from breast pocket
to buttocks until his flesh gaped
like a grim fish gill. We can cite the time
he called from a phonebooth outside Sam's
bar, doused in cheap neon, claimed blackjack
beatings had obliterated his brain. I recall,
too, the mid-morning crash that had allegedly
flipped his '48 Ford onto its back
and crushed his chest like a ripe cantaloupe,
compressed ribs like a bundle of kindling.

Drunk on Angel Breath

One Sunday afternoon, he smeared toothpaste
on a sofa cushion as evidence
of seepage from a brain concussion.
Such deception should have blackened his heart,
not catapulted him to a respectable, checkered-flag finish.

Now, there will be a lifelong silence
in the sound of his name. His death is
a tame detail that doesn't touch me anymore.

When the actual voice of death crawled
out of the phone, an electronic breath print
affirming demise, nullifying his former deaths,
I did not slump. I turned the page in the newspaper
I'd been reading, lay on the living room floor,

propped on an elbow, finally free of a dad who,
like a hungry wolf, hovered over us
ready to sink fangs into our haunted blood.

R. Nikolas Macioci

UNTROUBLED BY DAD'S DEATH

My biological dad died in Berea, Ohio.
I visited him only once after he moved
to the suburb of Cleveland, and during
that visit, his conversation consisted of
whimsical one-liners and exaggerated
pseudo facts. He said he was writing
a novel which he was not. I wanted
a serious exchange, always had, but
didn't know him to reach that level
of conversation. I never saw him again
after that visit, left thinking I was at fault
for not being a better son.
Often, I think of his grave
which I've never seen in person.
I don't remember how I acquired a picture
of it, but I have seen a photo. It's eerie
that the flat stone bears my exact name
since I'm a junior.

I did not see him during his final days.
If I had any heartbreak, it was intricate,
complex and didn't warrant mourning.
Even if his gravestone were close by,
I would be reluctant to pull weeds
after a rain or brush away fresh snow.
His abuse of Mom and me ripped
too deep a wound to palliate
with easy forgiveness. In this case,
I balk at the idea the dead deserve
our best attention.

DRINKING BEER LATE AT NIGHT

He pulls open the refrigerator door, grabs
a can of Bud Light, pops the tab, gulps
several swallows. He has just come from
the basement where he ironed five white shirts,
a week's worth of teaching garb. His aunt slumps
in her recliner, Alzheimer's asleep.

He stores his weekly six pack in the old
refrigerator relegated to the garage.
She doesn't know about his Friday night
binges, a secret ritual to sustain sanity
from being her sole custodian.

He guzzles five cans. Blurred vision distorts
the living room. He stumbles past her
slumped body, parts front-window drapes,
tries to focus on a late-night driver sloshing
rainwater from hissing tires. A neighbor's tomcat
hunches on the driveway, awaits an unlikely bird
at this hour. The mantle clock chimes once.

He snaps the tab on the last can. Foam wheezes
over his fingers. It's a lonesome sound. He has
a notion to stay up for indigo sunrise, but
tomorrow is Saturday, mowing day.
He has to sleep off this stupor.

On rubbery legs, he loses balance
toward the bedroom, slides onto the mattress
without pulling back the spread.
Pieces of himself separate from bones
as he slips into soothing sleep and away
from a caregiver's claustrophobic burden.

R. Nikolas Macioci

EVOCATION

Aunt Liz lives in a Lazy Boy recliner,
TV so loud I distinguish dialogue
through a closed, bedroom door. I teach,
so I have papers to grade. Since
she views the world through Alzheimer's,
I've learned not to leave her alone unless
necessary. I perch on the arm of a chair,
lean over the table that sits between us,
begin to mark essays. She warns of the people
she calls followers who constantly watch us,
glances out the window to secure safety.
I take a quick look over my shoulder.
The lawn needs mowed. Enough daylight
remains to complete the job before dark.
I push papers aside, trudge to the garage.

While I mow, she stands at the window
as if on guard, but I've learned enough
about Alzheimer's to know she's afraid
I'll abandon her.

It's late March. Darkness still comes early.
I switch on a floodlight attached to the top
of the garage. A lamp shines in the front
window. She continues to watch me. I smile
and wave. She waves back. As I finish,
I wonder which of us is more trapped.

Drunk on Angel Breath

She meets me at the back door leading
from garage into the house, turns, heads back
to her recliner. I resume paper grading,
think how decay and death are on the surface
of everything. She's ninety-four. Soon,
she will be gone. In the meantime,
I am her caregiver, and she owns me.

R. Nikolas Macioci

SURVIVOR'S WINDOW

I slump at a window in Grant Hospital.
Behind me, Aunt Liz lies comatose, infused
with morphine. The doctor says enjoy her
while you can. Hospice took over this morning.
It's raining. Drops look like electric pearls
against black, velvet night. An arrangement
of field flowers wilts nearby on a bedside cabinet.

I drop into an overstuffed chair,
stare at arms studded with needle marks,
eyes sealed with sedation. I sag at the window
again, hear wrist watch tick and the beep
of a monitor.

This is not the way to spend a Friday night,
waiting for someone to die. I'm stymied
there are no more possibilities. Soon,
someone will question whether or not neglected
flowers need watered, probably pitch them.

I turn to her, take a limp hand, hold it as if
personal contact could bring her back.
Rain slams the window. A blinding deluge
prevents me from seeing street or red
emergency sign.

I watch her chest as if I were an overseer of breath,
wait for the next one to be exhaled. Even
though I'm expecting the end, I'm surprised
when I see the terminal puff from her mouth.
I call the nurse, take a last look, and leave.

Drunk on Angel Breath

Rain has stopped. I retrieve my car, drive
onto wet street. Finality, an unwelcome presence,
rides along with me on the front passenger seat.

R. Nikolas Macioci

CANNING

When Aunt Liz died, she left thirty jars
of canned tomatoes on basement shelves.
Many of the jars were outdated. As
I emptied them down the disposal, it felt
like disrespect.

I used to linger near the sink to watch
her dice tomatoes, stir them in a porcelain
kettle, boil jars. She ground juice from
shriveled skins in a food mill. I tightened
jar lids as if they were never to be opened.
The whole process became yearly ritual
my aunts and mom followed like a religion.

When Aunt Liz's Alzheimer's advanced,
I assumed the task. I learned well, had
no problem putting up a significant number
of quarts. She watched and supervised.
It was her territory, and I was the interloper.
I didn't have the heart to stop the process
until she died, and then I gave away all
the paraphernalia. Nothing remains,
not a single thing.

PART TWO

"When the seasons shift, even the subtle beginning, the scent of a promised change, I feel something stir inside me. Hopefulness? Gratitude? Openness? Whatever it is, it's welcome."

Kristin Armstrong

 "The coming and going of the seasons give us more than the springtimes, summers, autumns, and winters of our lives. It reflects the coming and going of the circumstances of our lives like the glassy surface of a pond that shows our faces radiant with joy or contorted with pain."

Gary Zukav

"To be interested in the changing seasons is a happier state of mind than to be hopelessly in love with spring."

George Santayana

R. Nikolas Macioci

PREPARING FOR WINTER

Red oak leaves, like many little deaths,
peel from limbs, curlicue to the ground.
Over and over, repetition of loss loosens
from each branch, settles upon the grass.
Sky is blue silk and a flock of birds touch
amber sun with their wings.

I slump on a bench in Schiller Park, watch
enthusiastic walkers accumulate miles.
Landscapers rip out marigolds and begonias
as if they never mattered. Handfuls of fuchsia
fly to the flower heap. It appears as if
the world is being dismantled in preparation
for darker months.

Unafraid, geese gather on the walkway,
expect people to feed them. It feels wrong
I didn't bring bread or something. Minutes later,
they float on the pond out of reach.

A man and woman amble down the sidewalk
with their dog. I force myself to look at them.
I pretend I don't catch on to their romance as
I'm sad to be sitting on this bench by myself.

The geese suddenly return as if to collect
on a promise I can't keep. If they could talk,
I'd ask them if they are ever companionless
and what do they do on empty winter nights?

COLDNESS

Shrill winds drop temperatures to six
below zero. Moisture at the bottom
of windows, miniature bubble wrap,
measures an inch high. The furnace
hisses on with only a hint of warmth
to counterbalance chilled floors, walls.
The newscaster warns, "Bundle the kids.
Open doors under the sink, so pipes
don't freeze."

During the night, threatening winds
whipsaw the house as if it were a
wounded ship on a tumultuous sea.

Ice sculpts the oak tree
in the front yard to a glistening object
of art, glazes utility wires to appear
insulated in plastic.

The engine of an occasional car echoes
down the icy street as if the driver were
lost from any particular destination.

Tonight, blankets will be piled higher.
Street lamps will shine through pencil
tracings of frost on bedroom windows.
Tonight, cold, an invisible monstrosity
will clutch the city in its claw
and hold it there like a winter prisoner.

WINTERESQUE

Standing in a line beside icy sidewalk,
trees in Schiller Park are white-haired with snow.
The dark sun, hidden behind a curtain
of clouds, darkens more as the afternoon
dreams on. Automobiles inch along streets
like drowsy animals. On a steep hill,
kids slide down on homemade sleds.

Like a Siberian tiger, the beginning
of another snowfall prowls from dead-gray
sky. Foolhardy folks shovel walkways, slip
now and again in spite of rubber soles.
Snow increases a lacy drape suspended in air,
a silk screen of stars. Vision disappears
in a bone-colored whiteout. Stranded people
text everyone who matters. Everything
terrible in life becomes invisible.
It is the blossoming of a nothingness
as peaceful as the human body.

Snow continues throughout the night, but
morning shimmers under a touch of sun.
Blue as a Ming vase, plain sky canopies
the world grown white as a wedding gown.

WINTER WALTZ

If winter were a person,
he would take earth
in his arms and dance,
her leafless trees
against his shoulder,
an arm around
her dormant grasses,
a hand holding
a slender waist of sun.
They would whirl
on gravity's dance floor,
gliding in counts
of 1 2 3, 1 2 3.
She would throw
her head back,
counterbalancing
his weight. Their faces
iced with snow,
they would finish
the dance, earth curtsying,
winter bowing,
a gentleman
to the last minute of March,
she, a lady of spring's
watery cadenza.

AFTERWARD

Late Christmas night, the miracle fades.
A sterile residue of celebration sticks
to remaining hours like pieces of tape
on torn wrappings. Streetlight, mistaken
for moonlight, flows into the room
through a parted curtain. There is nothing
more to put away until next year. Clutter
of collapsed boxes piled on the hearth
catch fire from a kitchen match. It seems
as if deep silence has stopped everything,
guides me to a wingback chair I sag into
like a stringless marionette. I stare
at the lifeless room, lamps, tables, rug.
It's as if I'm waiting out my leftover life.
Like pieces of mica, stray bits of tinsel shine
from the carpet. I close my eyes, see again
tree's illumination now fuzzy recollection like
masthead lights from far-away, summer boats.

Soon, memory of this holiday will merge
with other Christmases, shrink in remembrance
to the size of a fingerprint, leaving, at best,
an elegant sadness.

R. Nikolas Macioci

IRISES

A line of thirteen purple irises grow
along the side of our garage
on Hinman Avenue, resemble
lavender ladies in frilly dresses.
Mom never picks them. I don't
even know if she planted them.

Maybe they came with the house.
They sag during these last days
of August. Their shadows lengthen

as sun drops lower. I break one
from a stem, press it open to see
if what goes on inside a dying

flower can be felt. Its limpness lies
on my nine-year-old fingers like dead silk.
I toss it to the ground, wonder

if flowers have an afterlife.

CREEPING PHLOX

Somewhat knotted,
it inches forward
each spring day
like purple ropes
of tinsel, spreading
along the terrace
to the rim
of the window well,
cascading over the metal
edge, a blanket
of lavender flowers
in suicidal gowns.

R. Nikolas Macioci

SUMMER DAY, 1913

It's Sunday, and ninety-four degree heat
brings a crowd to a favorite swimming
spot at the base of the Brooklyn Bridge.
Unclothed, the world of men and boys
is made of bare skin. Women come
in suits. Young mingle with old, drape
themselves atop granite walls and steel
girders. A group of boys stand shoulder
to shoulder on a dock, their bodies streaked
with sun and water drops. Modesty
is buried like a page in a closed book,
each giving the other invisible permission
to appear nude. No sadness surfaces
in this scene of relaxed serenity.
Even kids flex their bodies with joy,
understand that it is just a swim place
and not a place for arousal. Everything
is as it should be. The scene does not fall
short of an absolute absence of loneliness.
Talk is cordial, driven by camaraderie
in a mixture of tongues. There has to be
some kind of love here that people take
away some small part of when they return
home. For now, they want to enjoy
weak waves of water that lap pilings,
savor an afternoon of non-judgmental
escape.

ODE TO OHIO CORNFIELDS

For miles, monotony of cornfields, green
as gooseberry, stream by car windows.
Tassels blow in the wind like beachcombers'
yellow hair. Leaves, lofty scepters, rule
stalks deep into August soil, hide cobs
that sweeten by the hour. Soon enough,
moonlight will turn these stalks into eerie,
neck-tall phantoms.

Halfway to my destination, I'm still among
farm-size fields over which hawks and crows
screech garbled grammar. Row after row
of uniformity hypnotizes. Like a cyan cyclorama,
blaze of blue sky curves down behind the corn.

In a few weeks, combines will reap, thresh,
winnow, leave behind stubble of death.
I imagine the inevitable future of these crops,
most harvested to shanks and husks,
others attached to posts like pagan sacrifice
or made into decorative displays of demise
at roadside markets.

R. Nikolas Macioci

SEPTEMBER INSTEAD OF LOVE

The moon hangs like a sugar cube.
I amble the yard shirtless.
I'm never going inside again, I think.
Up there, cloud dunes resemble pyramids.
It is dangerous to be tempted
by hungry waves of a temperate night,
by moon's luminous edges that can cut
the heart. In short, I do not know
what is happening to me. I cross the yard,
circle back to stand beneath a trellis
of stars, guessing why this sterling flicker
of light feels so quaint, so old-fashioned,
quiet as holiness.

It is September and the season has started
to die. It is a time to put things away.
I have carried window screens to the basement,
stored the bird bath behind them near the furnace.
I have readied everything for the onslaught
of winter. Now, on one of those rare, balmy nights,
I'm walking the yard, listless as a railroad hobo
waiting for the next train ride to fulfillment.

AUTUMN AS LOVER

I'm lying in a hammock in the backyard.
It's an edgy, September day with a mix
of chill and warmth. I lie here in old age
as if I were following time's schedule.
Shifting stiff legs, I imagine I hear wind
squeak a door hinge. I sit up, but
there are no doors. Instead, bare branches
shimmer sunlight, and leaves wind down
from the dogwood tree, twisting, turning
like torn-out book pages. They drift
to the ground with their beautiful deaths.

There is a lesson to learn lying here
next to autumn, her brunette leaves curled,
her cloud face over mine. We have no secrets,
she and I. Arched over sunlight, she leans
her head against sky's back seat, breaking
open to seductive breezes, going limp
against shine of light that tastes her earlobes,
the black-veined body of demise radiant
between her thighs.

I turn my face to her sapphire skin,
and she releases birds hidden in her eyes.
She bends her face toward my lips
on this day of golden silhouettes, and we kiss,
once, so firmly it is truth that teaches me
the thing I went looking for is here:
implicit satisfaction to open my mouth
and receive the blue quiver of her tongue.

R. Nikolas Macioci

THE INEXPRESSIBLE RAPTURE OF AN AUTUMN DAY

Late September rain sobs on the windshield.
Wipers sweep away walls of water.
Leaf colors are faint and indistinct.
A sudden ribbon of sunlight streams from gray
clouds along sky's edges. The unexpected shaft
of golden light fans down to earth, and rain stops.

The whole sun creeps out, brightens yellow
sugar maples, red sourwood. I stop the car,
ogle intense tints and hues.

My grandma Mohr came from these hills.
She and my grandpa married on Potts Hill
in the Schmidt's, of sausage fame, house
a few miles from Bainbridge, Ohio.
I remember bringing Mom here.
She pointed to the window of the second-story
bedroom where her parents stayed.
Death has danced away my family, but
I'm lucky Mom showed me the past.

I start the car, turn onto a gravel road
where mascaraed leaves curl like magenta
and purple eyelashes, begin to blink
twilight shadows.

I drive back to the highway, think
sometimes an aimless journey is
the perfect trip.

TOWARD FALL

Among the oaks, incantations of leaves
are a chant, a crooning across the breeze
of something losing a hold. In the garden,
a string of aluminum pie pans brush
against each other making a metallic echo.
Like black needles, crows sew clouds onto cobalt
sky, careen and capture tops of elms.
Bees comb begonias, wings cloaked
in pollen. I amble toward the birdbath,
and when I reach it, September light shines
soft creases across my face on the water's
surface. I erase the lines with the full force
of the hose and watch water rain over
ceramic edges then level off like
a symmetrical puddle on a pedestal.
Above my head, dogwood foliage has become
brittle with crimson edges. Its leaves,
like simple truths, spiral to the ground forgotten.

A complex emotion brings me to a standstill,
leads to a moment of valuing everything:
the squirrel whose gaze follows me, the black
lab next door with its paws on the fence,
the sass of bluebirds on a telephone line.
All these entities remind me that I am
still able to walk away from death,
to live the fact of this day, bright and lush
as the shine of juice from a sliced apple.

R. Nikolas Macioci

OCTOBER FEELS LIKE A PLACE

It's where yellow leaves unfasten from birch
trees, and the smell of woodsmoke prevails.
It's a place near a pumpkin patch where
you turn the last page before winter.
It's crows on a cornfield fence rail, black
throats rattling caws. It's a place where
a profusion of chrysanthemums suddenly
mean more than any other flower.
It's where walking in leaves is absolute
contentment, where coming upon a hillside
of crayoned trees or leaving footprints
in early morning frost are surprise gifts.
It is a place where an enormous white moon
quickens the pulse, a place where nostalgia
gushes up from contemplation and throws
longing into gear. Mark October a place
where a multitude of bones, bats, and black
cats fill imagination with a flutter of welcome
fear, and you recoil from the rat-a-tat-tat
of a witch's fingernails on your window.
It's where roadside markets display a dozen
different baskets of apples, and jugs of cider,
the color of sunset, become broth of the season.
Let someone special stand in this place with you.
Let leaves fall around you both and feel
nothing less than love.

THE WORLD STUNNED BY LEAVES

I awaken to leaves withering
outside. It will be the warmest day
in October. I glance at relentless blue
sky unblemished by cloud but scratched
with trails of jet exhaust. My heart
grows wild with longing. The leaves trick me
into melancholy. I don't know why,
and I don't know what I want exactly,
but I want it more than I've ever wanted anything.
I turn back into the room, totter into clothes,
ready to rake beneath the giant oak.
Next door, a neighbor burns what he has gathered.
I inhale acrid smoke as bitter as memory,
a time spent stumbling out of a relationship.
I rake the leaves wearing the blush of red.
Air crisp as an edge of paper, sharp as a thorn.
I breath deeply, exhale from beneath my heart.
No flaws mar this day of smooth sunshine
soaking a sweatshirt, warming the skin
like the touch of new romance. I bag the leaves,
brittle, crackling crumbles in my hands.
For a long time, I stand still holding the rake,
searching corners of thought for how being
alive feels when I've been ankle-deep
in remnants of death.

OCTOBER IS WHAT I AM

Autumn drapes thinner light over burning
bushes that have already turned lipstick red.
Gold coinage of elm and purple plumage
of sourwood bespeak how death entombs
elegance. Even if I weren't a romantic,
I would say my blood has turned to woodsmoke,
made me the cornfield scarecrow waiting
for shadowy birds to land on my shoulders,
transform me into one of a million pumpkins
in a ten-acre field. Becoming autumn
is not a feat. It is a furious longing
I can only begin to satisfy by identifying
with a sundial and letting leaves tremble
across my surface. I might lift myself
into the air as an umbrella and catch
early October drizzle, moreover, what makes
me want to be the harvest moon, orange
as a rusted medallion or chrysanthemums
yellow as corn on the cob. I am
slow to accept that I cannot become this
season, so, afflicted by nostalgia, I lean
an elbow on the windowsill, stare at
spiraling leaves and that moon again large
as an airplane. I ache from falling in love
with fall, a wistful hunger for the unnamable
that almost kills me for wanting it.

AUTUMN WOMAN

Maple leaves flutter in October breeze
like yellow finches. The sun buttons
to a burnished blue sky. As she walks
along the sidewalk into town, the day
seems to bulge with silver light. Corn shocks
and scarecrows are fastened to lampposts
like pagan sacrifices. A scourge of leaves
whirl around her ankles as if scoffing
at spinsterhood. A red neon sign
announces the flower shop open.
The maniacal grin of a jack o' lantern
welcomes her. When she opens the door,
the tinkle of a bell accompanies her inside.
The scent of eucalyptus pervades the air.
Large pots of rust-colored chrysanthemums
populate the space below a counter
of ceramic pumpkins. She greets
the proprietor with a slight quiver.
So daylight doesn't stumble across her skin
of seventy-one years, she keeps her back
to the windows. Choosing a small bouquet
of mums, orange as the last wisps of sunset,
she stiffens, steps to the exit. Outside, holding
her purchase to her chest, she embraces it.

R. Nikolas Macioci

OF AUTUMN

I've known this kind of death before,
leaves falling upon window sills,

their brittle spines clicking against glass.
August sun, like the highest apple

in the tree, blinds when I look upward.
Soon, I will blow away cold with breath

in my hands. Soon, surfaces will be
erased by snow. In the meantime,

on such a blue-sky day, a murder
of crows settles like cornfield ghosts

on a farmer's fenceposts. Wind pulls
down more leaves, dances across

open spaces. I will reply
to oncoming winter with fires and locks

on frozen doors. Inside now, I stare
out the window at my dogwood tree,

its limbs mostly bare, admit I am helpless
against change, for instance, the beginning

of morning's dew-lacquered grass,
the season's spill of leaves.

AUTUMN PARLORS

You have not known love tender as a shiver
of wheat blown by a hint of breeze.
If I could, I would loosen you from years
of controlled hands, let them seek, reach,
clothe, and collapse deep within another
person's warmth. Yours is refined cruelty,
a frosted life self-imposed. Birds are all
that come near you, dancing stiffly, picking
at jewel-colored leaves like spinsters sorting
patterns of loneliness in their autumn parlors.

A NOVEMBER LIFE

Diane has taken up knitting.
She sags in an occasional chair
by the casement window. The mantel
clock tick-tocks language of lost hours.
Late afternoon sun makes transparent art
on hardwood floor.

She's seventy-two, doesn't know how
to dismiss the thought she has nothing
to expect but death.

She reads Shakespeare, listens to Mahler,
makes ceramic Christmas trees. Once,
she had a romantic relationship with a man
named Paul. They had worked together
in the state office building downtown where
she handled clerical tasks. He was her supervisor.
She wasn't prepared for love to tire so soon.

"Men" she thinks, "are never as present
as they appear to be, roving among detritus
of their own egos."

Autumn light becoming less, she places
her knitting on a side table, wraps a coat around her
shoulders. Outside, on the back patio, she breaks bread
for birds, stands still, watches sunset dissolve.

After sun has cooled, she ambles back inside,
snaps on a lamp that throws a circle of light
on the table. Unfinished knitting lies within the glow.

ULTIMATE AUTUMN

Oak leaves spiral like spring blossoms in reverse,
golden as the bracelets found in Tutankhamun's
tomb. Yellow ash leaves shiny as a lynx's eyes,
maple red as a heated fire tong twist from branches
and curl downward. All night, trees are changing
from green to purple, black, pink, magenta, and
blue like Joseph's coat spread over an entire forest.
Sassafras, orange as rusted train wheels, stand
among chartreuse sweetgum. Black tupelo is
harbinger of all colors on a single branch. It is the
jewel against blue rockfish sky. The forest's paint
exploded, and a universe of color dripped to daub
each leaf. Flamboyant, vibrant, as a court jester's cap,
hues and shades of coloration caress death,
cascade from decay. Such beauty is the counterfeit
forgery of life, the seasonal loadstone that attracts
wonderment and awe. So much color distracts
from empty branches left behind like abandoned lives
or the carapace of a cold relationship.

R. Nikolas Macioci

NEGOTIATING THE LAST DAY OF NOVEMBER

Early dusk bespeaks the clock's new hours.
A heavy wind combined with gloom foretells
a storm is on the way. It could be rain slicing
at windows or whirlwinds of snow.

Dogwood branches bob with each capricious
gust. Cedar limbs thrash up and down
like green feather dusters. Right now,
weather is a lawless rogue with whip in hand,
black cape flapping wild. It is twilight
on the edge of frost, a hint of winter
with its blustery howls.

Shadows climb walls like phantom guests
who have come in uninvited. It is a night of
impoverished warmth, a time to pull a wingback
chair near fire and drowse within kindled light,
while a blaze of logs releases a scribble of sparks.

PAINTING A NOVEMBER MOOD PIECE

It is a cold train rail in winter,
on a near coatless day in mid-November.
My body refuses to move far from
a blanket, and sky, is a snow field
waiting to happen. When I open the door
a riot of leaves whirl at my feet. Birds
are scarce, and trees tremble a network
of twigs. Sun has abandoned the world
outside my window. A uniform bleakness
becomes the landscape where shrieking
geese reverberate.

I bend over my desk, press pen to paper.
Wind announces itself outside the window
whipping bare branches. There is a lulling
effect to my loneliness. Preferable
to a crush of people, I choose the fragility
of empty rooms. Face over the legal pad,
words for a poem slip to the printed line.

Satisfied, I walk through the house, look
down basement steps, listen for unusual
sounds. The furnace clicks on like a soothing
ballad. I sit in an overstuffed chair reading,
eyes heavy with the sweetness of sleep.
Wind flicks leaves against the windows.
Finally, there is no conspicuous choice
but to lean back, close my eyes.

R. Nikolas Macioci

WHAT TO SAY AND FEEL IN AUTUMN

Maple leaves, red quilt pieces, lie beneath
the tree. A light breeze sews them together.
If it could talk, the tree would be indifferent
to loss.

I forget language, look past words at an
inexpressible day of sky blue as Crater Lake.
A rage of sun, banana-skin yellow, sculpts
landscape in dazzling light. These are
my thoughts as I let go of the last hours
of summer and prepare for first frost.

I count down days in the last week
of September, remember driving
to southern Ohio on blue days like
today, cruising by farm fields full
of apricot-colored pumpkins.

At this moment I'm in my backyard
with a peck basket gathering apples
groundhogs haven't eaten. It is a sad tree
that has become skeletal. Soon, I will
call a tree service and have it cut down.
The smell of its innermost wood will
permeate the air, and I will breathe in
nostalgia, picture the day Mom planted it
twenty years ago. For now, I watch
its leaves collect on the ground,
crackling under my feet like cellophane.

AT THE FESTIVAL OF THE LEAVES

Sun tangles in trees. Its cat's cradle
floods my windshield. I am driving
among hills of southern Ohio on Route 56
toward Bainbridge, a town small enough
to put a fence around. My destination
draws me out to view aspen yellow as
amber, rust of black tupelo, scarlet
sassafras.

I park several blocks on the outskirts
because town's people are meandering
in droves. Booths, shops, street vendors
offer everything from sandwiches to furniture,
socks to hand-carved canes. Humming
under my breath, I watch people watching
people. Life is simple. Since my parents
died, I have lived without anyone, so I stroll
the sidewalk, ice cream in hand, craving
a companion.

Just for fun, I pay a boisterous young man
to guess my age and weight. It costs three
dollars, and he's wrong in either case. My
prize is a necklace with two interlocking hearts.

R. Nikolas Macioci

PART THREE

"The family is one of nature's masterpieces."

George Santayana

R. Nikolas Macioci

THE RELUCTANT HUNTER

Uncle Peck shot a quail with superior accuracy
and called it sport. It was disillusioning
to see him search his pouch for another cartridge
as if one shot-down bird wasn't enough.
It was the beginning of autumn and cold,
flickering leaves, yellow, orange, red,
colors seen in most fires, twisted from trees.

 I was staying the weekend with him and his wife,
Aunt Sarah, and although they had five children,
in and around my age of nine, none seemed
interested in this activity.

He had invited me to go with him
to learn to hunt. Gunless, but eager for adventure,
I followed him out the door. I never had any interest
in learning to hunt, but it made me feel older
to accept his invitation. In fact, I hated the idea
of killing anything.

We continued to tramp over corn-stubbled field.
Occasionally, a ring-neck pheasant revealed
its hiding place and that bird, too, suffered
my uncle's bullet. With his gun in hand,
any creature became prey regardless
of the season. He didn't own hunting licenses.
The field he stalked lay only a block
from his house. It was 1950,
and surrounding territory remained rural.
The possibility of being apprehended
without a license was remote.

Satisfied with his catch, we started home.
I couldn't keep up with his long strides,
felt like his trailing shadow, slightly embarrassed
to have rejected fulfillment from killing.

UNCLE BOB

During last hours of his life, he asked
to have his feet rubbed. This is the uncle
who only came to visit when he was
drunk, belligerent, argumentative,
and wanted to fight.

Now, he lies on a crumpled bedsheet,
pugnacity gone, strains for last breath
from lungs at war with bacterial
pneumonia. Nurses become the
government in the room, regulating
machines to avert death.

Family members gather near
the bed, moment to moment wither
into acceptance that the benefit of doubt
has been taken away. It is as if they watch
a magic show when the magician fails
to pull a rabbit from a hat.

The room is made of whispers.
This is a time when even the water glass
on the bedside stand becomes a reminder
of options of the living, commentary
on the mundane.

When death delivers Bob's last breath,
a nurse attempts to close eyes.
They remain reluctant until her third try.

Family stare at the body, each other,
the floor, and then, at nothing
particular.

THE ROUNDHOUSE

When I was a kid, Mom often drove
her '51 yellow Mercury to Johnson's
restaurant on South Parsons Avenue,
directly across the street from a train
building called the roundhouse. It
was semicircular and reminded my
pre-adolescent mind of an angel food
cake cut in half. The building sat
atop an embankment and was used
to store and service locomotives.
She told me her dad used to paint
letters on train cars there for B&O
Railroad until he went blind. She
would tell me this every time we
went to Johnson's. She said he was
the best painter who worked there
and did it all freehand, no stencils.
Whenever I heard these words, I
would sit a little straighter, feel
pride that Grandpa Mohr had the
touch of an artist who painted
words on railroad cars that traveled
as far away as the Appalachian
Mountains. Mom made it sound
like the roundhouse was a family
monument to which I owed respect.

Seventy-one years later, I don't live
in the South End of Columbus, Ohio
anymore. I dwell in the small town
of Groveport, about fifteen minutes
from Columbus, and I only pass
the roundhouse occasionally. Its
windows are broken, waist-high
weeds proliferate, and the building
itself is crumbling, vacant, and useless
as the words he once put into motion.

GRANDPA MOHR

Blindness did not deter him from shuffling
every day down the path along the canal
at Buckeye Lake to Harry's Bar for a few
beers, white cane, a gift from the Lions
Club, extended in front of him like a giant
ant feeler. Perpetual attire consisted of
shirt, pants, Romeo slippers and soiled
cardigan. He smelled slightly of urine.

Returning to the cottage, he slid tiny steps
forward until he nudged his Naugahyde
recliner, dropped onto the seat and exhaled
a sigh. Then he would close his eyes,
merely a formality, and sleep.

I used to stand nearby, stare at work-worn
hands and wait for him to awaken. He never
hugged or shook hands with me. His touch
had replaced light and was only a tool against
wrong turns and guesses.

The man who took careful steps to his chair
used to walk a herd of cattle fifty miles
from Bainbridge, Ohio to Columbus. Later
in life, he painted letters on railroad cars
at the roundhouse in Columbus, ran a farm
tractor after he came home from painting,
sometimes into the night, and helped to raise
ten kids with perfect table manners.

R. Nikolas Macioci

Seventy years later, I stand in my garage
on Frebis Avenue, wrap fingers around his
shovel and hoe, hoist them to my shoulder
and head toward the garden. I will break soil
in his memory.

A HALF DOZEN MIRRORS

Aunt Ada, early in her marriage, saved
money for mirrors. She hung six
in the living room, surrounded herself
with selves. They encircled her
with affirmative reflections. Sometimes,
when I would visit, she would ask me
to clean the mirrors, a job I hated, but
I would climb the couch or the chair
to reach silvered surfaces, ignoring
my own reflection.

She was a good-looking woman, but
I suspected below her consciousness
lay ceaseless insecurity. Leaning
in a doorway or standing at the stone mantle,
she trusted repetition of looking at herself
to yield an attractive face. To be around
her, a person would never think she was vain,
but in her house of mirrors, vanity flourished.
She was good-hearted beyond compare, and
her self-admiration was less a fault than
a convenient way to validate existence. Often,
she would glance toward the gilded frames,
never touching her image for fear of leaving
a smudge or a fingerprint.

After she died, the mirrors were sold
in a yard sale for a pittance. People ogled
the frames, carried them to their cars,
ignorant of my aunt's ghost that still shown
like an invisible memory out of the polished glass.

BLACK LAMB

Mom and I have traveled to her sister's twelve-acre
spread in Dayton, Ohio to spend Thanksgiving day.
I'm eight, bored by adult company, so
I amble to the barn on Aunt Clara's property
to feed the only animal, a lamb named Bingo.
I pull a handful of grass tangled in barbed wire
fence. The lamb, black as obsidian, a wool shadow,
ears pricked, runny nose, mosies to me.
Pink-tongued, the lamb chews the grass from my hand.

Overhead, dense, gray clouds hover like an implied
insinuation of rain. Lightning, a jagged piece of white
silk, snags sky. Thunder follows, lightning's handmaiden.
Intermittent flashes slash through fading light of afternoon.

A bell around Bingo's neck gossips
the lamb's whereabouts as the animal turns
toward the barn, away from me and ripped air.

Behind me, my aunt's two-story stone house
assures safety from the storm. I climb cement
steps to the pillared porch, enter on hardwood
floors, welcome a fire, redder than bricks, on the grate.

At the dinner table, I slump from a melancholy
memory of the lamb's sudden bolt to safety,
the hollowness of it's receding bell, and the fact
that I could not bring it inside away from the blue rain.

ALCHEMY FOR MOM

I stand before her, a purveyor of pills,
hold court with her constant ailments.
What passes for her life amounts to
periods of perpetual recovery.
She rants after swallowing blood
pressure medicine or the capsule
that saves her heart. She carps about
the other fourteen tablets ingested
each morning. Standing at the kitchen
sink, holding a half-peeled banana,
she watches white, dogwood blossoms
unfurl more each day. Stirring a cup
of instant coffee constitutes the last
step in her morning ritual before she drops
into a well-worn rocker.

R. Nikolas Macioci

She wrinkles so easily, day after day,
comes apart, stooped, wincing from hip pain
where bone rubs against bone. Odds militate
against the life she wants, so she settles
for spending most of the day in her chair.
Sometimes, she wonders aloud what will be
her demise: cancer, stroke, or heart attack.
Will she become a chemo target, the recipient
of lung treatment, or paralyzed to immobility?
Her sister had pulmonary fibrosis, friable tissue,
often coughed up blood. Mom embraces
the possibility of convalescence, always
said we inherit bad health. She also said
it's a shame we can't put on a special hat
that would guarantee a second youth.

Mom's ninety-four years pushes death aside
every day, lives on the threshold of cure
she says drifts into her veins like intravenous
hope. Stubborn as a stain, if she were compelled
to undergo surgery, she would embrace
the possibility of recovery, dazzle herself
by her body's demand to recuperate.
From farm stock, her tough constitution throws
dishwater on the fires of defeat, accepts,
with humble thankfulness, fate's gift of longevity.

SLEEPING MOTORCYCLES

My cousin nudges me toward his workspace,
a large area in a warehouse-type building
where an artist's studio, print shop, and
two apartments exist.

Over years, he amassed fourteen motorcycles,
none of which is drivable because
all of them have been disassembled.
Like broken ghosts, frames of Kawasakis,
Indians, Yamahas, Suzukis, and Triumphs
weigh against each other on the ground.
Others loom on makeshift shelves.
Work benches and tables overflow
with engine components and intake parts,
everything necessary to make cycles complete.

Years ago, when he had a workable chopper,
he and his wife sped along rural roads
until the day they skidded. He sustained
a few scratches, but she flew from her seat,
landed face first in gravel. They rushed
to the emergency room. Plastic
surgery restored her looks, but they never
went riding together again.

My eyes roam the area. I tell him
the cycles look like they nap, wait for him
to awaken them in their original form.
He says arthritis won't allow long work-hours,
claims someday he'll put them all back together
and sell them.

R. Nikolas Macioci

As a kid, he built things and took things apart.
I told him these metal frames and accessories
form a piece of nostalgia he doesn't want to lose.
He did not disagree, but picked up a carburetor
from a nearby table, looked at it
like he was on the edge of discovery,
put it back as though he wanted to keep quiet
about the future.

UNCLE HEINE'S WORLD

First, flowers impressed him most, daffodils
unfurling lemon petals in pools of spring
sunshine, hundreds of tulips in meticulous rows,
opening like kaleidoscopic cups. Soon,
however, Uncle Heine became partial
to vegetable gardening. Tomatoes, corn, beans,
and cabbage flourished. All summer long,
he supplied family and neighbors with produce.
Eventually, he built a cold frame for strawberries,
hinged two, abandoned, storm doors to the frame
to let in light. He loved to feel his hands in soil.

During all the years he tended the estate,
he also held a full-time job. Uncle Heine
and his wife, Aunt Ada, labored
at Federal Glass Company. She retired
after twenty-five years. He died
of a heart attack one month short of being
on the job fifty years.

It was three-shift employment.
When Aunt Ada worked nights, I rode with him
to pick her up. Over time, she managed to pilfer
enough glassware in her lunchbox to supply all
six of her sisters, three brothers with glasses,
plates, and bowls. No one in the family thought
of it as theft. They believed it amounted to
borrowing for a lifetime.

Uncle and aunt are gone now. What was once
a lovely, immaculate estate lies in ruins.
Their house sold to a neglectful couple.
Weeds proliferate two-and-a-half acres
devoid of flower and vegetable gardens,
a ramshackle place where wisteria girdles trees
and strawberries no longer grow.

ORIENT

It's rumored my aunt opened a bedroom window
in midwinter when Chris was a baby and
he caught pneumonia which led to encephalitis.
The baby lived and grew, but many doctors and
examinations later generated a hopeless verdict
that the child would never be right.
Talk of a sanitarium ensued. The parents winced
at such an idea, remembering the '40s movie,
The Snake Pit in which Olivia de Haviland portrays
a character writhing in a lunatic asylum.
The caseworker assured them times had changed.

Chris became a lifetime resident in a home
for the mentally challenged. Aunt and uncle never failed
to visit every week until Chris died in his late 60s.

He loved to sit on my uncle's lap.
When he reached maturity, Chris continued
to perch on his dad's knees.

I never met Chris, but I heard about him
all my life, finally saw him at his viewing.
In the coffin, he appeared handsome
and fragile as a glass figurine.

His parents kept careful watch at The Orient,
and though Chris lived within a limited space,
he never had to endure white walls
of an old-fashion sanitarium. My uncle said
he knew The Orient wasn't a perfect place.
He had heard residents voices slur reality,
talk to the cul-de-sac of uninterested ears.
He also said it didn't matter which exotic street
you packed your bag from because we all end up
in our own kind of institution.

My uncle claimed that when he reached his car
after each visit, sky loomed behind him
like a statement of loss.

When I think of Chris, I think of his dad holding him,
maybe rocking him in a sentimental rhythm.
Chris couldn't talk. He made mumbling sounds.
My uncle tried to teach him to recognize his name,
but year after year, when Chis's dad called his son's name,
Chris was permanently absent.

PART FOUR

"We become not a melting pot but a beautiful mosaic. Different people, different beliefs, different yearnings, different hopes, different dreams."

Jimmy Carter

R. Nikolas Macioci

DRUNK ON ANGEL BREATH

The moon glows so bright Paul can see a man
race over crusted snow, swinging arms
as if any second the man might lose
his lead on the edge of light. Frosted glass
separates Paul from a pine tree in the front
yard on which old snow has frozen into a sheen
of white stars. On this glazed night, passing
cars whisper slush. Across the street, tubular
neon burns the words "Buddy's Bar."

The radio predicts another imminent storm.
Kneeling on the hearth, he strikes a kitchen
match, ignites logs behind wire mesh. Flames
bloom upward. Andirons gleam. He slips back
to the window, sees new snow flicker down
under vapor light. In the parking lot
of the neighborhood bar, stumps of cars protrude
from mounds of white. The bar door opens.
A young man and a giggling girl fall
against each other. Their lopsided steps snake
a path to the nearest car. They fall-lean
against the hood. He lifts her, holds her
against himself. Her jacket slips up, shows skin
the boy reaches for. Hands beneath her blouse,
his fingers climb warmth. Atop the hood,
they curve down until his head touches
the windshield, and she is pressed against him,
glistening with desire not unlike Paul's own.

Paul closes the drapes across their inebriated dance,
splashes his throat with a double shot of Angel Breath
gin, turns off lamps. His shadow from firelight haunts
a wall, face flushed from whiskey and firelight.
Swallowing more and more liqueur, Paul sees
a chair disappear, then the couch. The carpet floats
up to balance his feet. His brain obliterates
sensation, but for sound of a revving
engine tucked within distance.

It is silent in the room except for blazing
wood popping orange syllables from its throat.
Paul folds to the hearth, his body parallel
to fire. Hands at sides, splays of autumn reds
and yellows robe his shoulders. He nods
at leafy light, struggles to his knees
for another swig. Back to the steel window
frame, cold as a corpse, he stares unfocused
at ground outside, uncontrollable speed
swirling his brain in circles.

Drunk on Angel Breath

Turning back to the living room, he buckles
to knees, fans his palms over carpet
as if looking for lost coins in high grass.
What he finds is a mutable weapon
much like a fire poker lying not far from the grate.
He holds it against his chest, presses it
until bones ache, then slides back
to the floor, synapses comatose.
Up on knees again, he crawls back
to the window, raises himself to its ledge.
The neighborhood bar is dark now.
His hand flutters toward snow-deadened sound
of a passing car, beckons to the possibility
that one more jogger will run along street-lit
sidewalk, or that a car will turn into his driveway,
flash welcoming headlights through the window.
He lifts an arm above his head, holds it
there, lowers it, shaping a gun from thumb
and finger. He aims the gun
between his lips, and this is how he murders
Saturday night, leaving himself
satisfied to glimpse a shimmer of death
against the heat of intoxication and snow.

R. Nikolas Macioci

LIBRARY EPILOGUE

Homeless, he slouches at a wooden table
in the reference room, Columbus
Dispatch open in front of him, an excuse
for being there. Fluorescent light glares
over newsprint he mostly ignores.
It is almost closing time. He returns
the paper, drags himself toward the door.
Last orchestral notes echo
from the audio-visual room. A blast
of finale, frenzy of sounds remind him
of teaching music before layoff,
poverty, and no housing forced him
to the streets. Leaving, he trudges
past a showcase displaying Shawnee
artifacts, a bit of history about which
he is indifferent.

Bronze doors lock behind him, tight as
a secret. Night surrounds like
an inescapable hand. July evenings
make it easy for him to sleep
outside wherever he can. Plodding
down Grant Avenue, he passes wishless
faces, familiar comrades struggling
to stay alive.

As a child, his parents turned him away,
tortured him with abandonment
and foster care. Now, he blesses beauty
of skies, lives within safety of sadness,
is burned raw from the stars.

AMY LOWELL AND I

I would have taken up cigar smoking
to have been friends with Amy Lowell.
I would even have fussed with Ezra pound.
I'd be tempted, though, to transform her bun
into a 1920's bob and blatantly denounce
the epithet of Hippopoetess.
I would revere her image-i-nation,
defend her absence of line breaks.
She, Ada Dwyer Russell, and I would travel
to England, but I would not peep into
their romantic interludes. We would laugh
a lot at ourselves and at those poets
who straight-jacket themselves
into metrical constraint. We would linger
all afternoon over a bottle of Hennessy brandy
We would puff, drink, talk and read poetry
to one another. I would ignore
masculine features that gave her such despair
in school and relish her straightforward,
opinionated mind. We would argue
over little things but never big things
such as love, death, and immortality.
If I could, I would carry her posthumous
Pulitzer Prize to her gravesite, sit down in front
of the tombstone and say, "Amy, you did it.
You lived a beautiful life."

R. Nikolas Macioci

MY BEST EFFORT TO LEARN ABOUT DEATH

At first, there's a hint of tears and then her voice
over the phone loses its purpose, and she sobs.
It's like a terrible homework assignment to think
what to say. I utter usual clichés, think better of it,
and stop. When it comes to death, understanding
is done. Her sister, a few houses away, clutches
at life, resists cancer's conquest. Thanksgiving
is a month away, and it is doubtful that this sister
will be attending family dinner. I, too, have been
through this kind of loss. In fact, I wrote a poem
years ago called "The New Thanksgiving" in which
I portray that special day without family. After
talking with my friend, I felt compelled to create
a poem that would plummet the depths of death,
let me know once and for all how to deal with it.

I did not produce such word magic. No miracle
surfaced to let me go behind the brick wall
that separates the living from the dead. I did not
comfort her. She, an autumn tree without leaves,
a bare, broken tree, was whipped by winds of grief,
and I failed to make things better for her.

Before I stop writing, I want the reader to know
I won't try again to explain what happens
to the mind during extreme sadness when
all that are left are an empty chair, the scent
of a handkerchief, and the memory-echo of
Death passing with a loaded coffin.

THE ICE ODOR OF BONE

The pilot swallows a gutful of fear.
The Boeing 777X burns downward.
Fire started smaller than a fingernail,
splintered to a handful of brightness
June white. He's frantic, drunk on disbelief,
the moment, a mockery of order.
He thinks of death, the yellow dust
of cremation. Everything checked out
on takeoff: auxiliary fuel pump, flight
controls, instruments and radios. He
did nothing wrong. Bad luck has splashed
into his blood like a destructive kiss.
The plane noses through damaged clouds
toward Knoxville, sweeps heaven aside
as if it were imagination's bad idea.
The pilot loses dimension after dimension,
continues to clutch the yoke, sweats
chill of being on stage in a final scene.
The plane, a costly dream, coils earthward
away from a tiny, white pearl of sun.
The pilot gulps air, his throat dry
as cactus, swallows inevitable truth
that strangles light.

R. Nikolas Macioci

THE ORGANIST

In a white shirt and light-blue trousers, you lean
over the keyboard, fingers selecting notes
that hang in the air, excite your connection
between music and sex. You want to remove
your clothes as you said you had once done
in a belfry-like room hidden from the congregation,
your penis growing with each stroke and vibration.

Today, you are clothed and pure
to the eye, play like an expert typist,
find keys as easily as you would a lover in the dark.
You have memorized arrangements for weddings
and High Mass, said that while you play
you are certain eyes of the priest massage your back,
lay small touches on your shoulders, invite you
to show him how to rid himself of forbidden ardor.
This is the way you go about your work, fondle
the urge to tell him all you know about impure
flesh and impulse.

On the way home, a secret hunger spreads
from belly to bones. You cruise past McDonald's
drive-thru window, order a hamburger, park,
tilt back your seat, and stare through the windshield
at empty branches and fallen leaves.

Drunk on Angel Breath

WHAT PEOPLE IN NEW YORK CITY KNOW ABOUT SUMMER

Somewhere, children count off numbers for street games.
Women launder sheets, slide windows open
to see who strolls alleyways. Local liquor stores
wrap Muscatel in brown paper bags. Sun, on a rotisserie
of sky, scorches sidewalks, beams into cramped
apartments.

A thousand trucks with identical exhaust pollute
flower vendors, wither bouquets wrapped in tissue paper
green as death. Grass competes with concrete. Pigeons
strut for a handout, ascend to heights of unsatisfied hunger.
Lunch-hour handball courts shine luminous sweat
and Coca-Cola smiles. Executives break from hollow-eyed
secretaries, bicycle stationary miles to the next machine.
An entire city obeys laws of madness, like medicine
you respect if it helps you feel better. The habit
of making excuses to derelicts who damn you for looking
so fit and living well, for withholding their chance to
guzzle

cheap whiskey. You cross streets, pause on corners
beside fathers in tank undershirts and old ladies
with shriveled faces. Tonight, a boiling breeze
from the river stifles breathing, but, nevertheless,
couples stroll on the edge of ancient intimacy, kiss,
wait for the tallowy moon to come from far away
and cool their faces. You sit down on a bench.
The jawbone of moon opens its bright light on you, too.
Boat lights illuminate water. Shadows lull you
to forget streets only several blocks south where
the homeless, at the bottom of a hierarchy of fate,
roll up in cardboard boxes because stars do not
beat their light down on the unfortunate. Even

at midnight, factory smoke bullies clouds.
Freeways roar a continuous scream of tornadic speed,
You say you couldn't move away, as people in movies
always do, to the country or at least to one of 10,000
identical homes in the suburbs? You catch a late subway car

with enough graffiti to be a circus act, gape
at the parade of characters, stooped, boisterous, lame.
You wait to see if you will ride all the way,
take your chance on a destination.

THIBAUDET PLAYS THE THIRD MOVEMENT FROM SAINT SAENS' PIANO CONCERTO NO. 5

He pounds opening notes with determination
of a blacksmith at an anvil. Throughout
the Molto Allegro, his fingers dance
toward the middle section. Affection
for the piece possesses the piano.

The conductor's baton pokes, slices air
in every direction. Like Excalibur
pulled from the stone, his baton flawlessly
conveys the composer's intent.

The blur of Thibaudet's hands, frantic birds,
hammer out the final theme as fast as
spontaneous sound will allow.
His blond hair, handsome face belie
youth he is long past, but his energy
reigns beyond doubt. Building
to the crescendo, he devours the keyboard
with passion, delivers a finale
that brings the audience to its feet.

Exiting the stage, he climbs stairs beyond view.
Insistent applause brings him back down steps
to the front of the stage. The audience cheers.
He repeats the routine twice more before
listeners settle into satisfied silence.

In the wings, he wipes sweat from his brow
with the back of his hand, embraces
his long-term partner, Paul,
as if they were part of one body.

THIS MAN, THIS SONG

It's Friday night. My neighbor stumbles
around his backyard, steering clear of
a life he doesn't want to see,
builds avoidance beer after beer, then stops,
slurs high-school, football memories
over chain-link fence. I amble toward him.
His middle-age belly presses against
rusted links. He asks if I want a beer.
I decline. His flushed face looks empty,
lost as it does every weekend
during these binges. Like a magician
out of control, he has turned his mind
to either mush or stone.

Often, from my bedroom window,
I have watched him prance from wall to wall
in his garage while his wife slouches
on an aluminum, folding chair, the one beside it
remaining empty.

A glance at his house, and I see his wife
staring out the kitchen window, watching
his weekend obliteration. He continues
to reminisce about his high school football
coach, his admiration of the intolerance
the coach had for undisciplined players
and wayward students in general.
"He was tough, and didn't take no shit
from nobody."

Drunk on Angel Breath

July moon has risen above trees
bordering our yards. His wife snaps
on a floodlight attached to the back
of their house as if she suspects too much
intimacy between the men at the fence.
Having had enough of his wasted hours,
I say I'm going inside, turn away, feel
I've left a small child playing in the street,
looking up at chrome stars, oblivious
of oncoming vehicles.

R. Nikolas Macioci

A SIDELONG LOOK AT AN AGING WOMAN IN A CHAIR IN A NURSING HOME

I've arrived for my weekly visit
with Sandy Ditschle, a friend
from teaching days. Each time I appear,
the same woman lounges in the same chair

near the front door. When she's been awake,
I've stopped and chatted, learned some things
about her life. Today, however, like a puppet
with no more performances, she surrenders,

droops head as if to hear intimate words,
nods into sleep, a practiced death pose.
Sisters and brothers deceased, when she awakens,
she awakens to no one to come back to.

I amble past her, note sallow skin, flaccid
features as if her face has been attached
to a tension string that someone let go of.
Her eyelids, sockets, cheeks, mouth, chin

have loosened forward, spilled upon her
chest toward a nap. She looks as if
she's taken a last breath. I stroll onward,
head toward Sandy's room, everything

about the old lady pressing into my heart
like a handful of needles.

BURN

Mom and I slouch in the burn unit
of Children's Hospital. I reached across
a gas-stove burner, and my bathrobe sleeve
caught fire. When I glance up, paramedics
wheel in a four-year-old girl. I'm four years
older, hear a nurse say the youngster's charred
skin results from house fire hotter than the core
of the earth. The kid screams as doctors and
nurses surround her charred body. The tongue
of her pain cries out again. Her family arrives,
plops onto plastic chairs across from us.
Their panic-stricken faces beg for
information. Mom whispers *probably
even the touch of air on the child's skin hurts.*
Another shriek from behind the curtain stabs
our ears. We hear uprush of movement, frantic
maneuvers, but no more howls from the child.

A doctor, head bowed, sags from behind
the curtain, voice reluctant with failure.
Family members jump from seats, whip
the curtain aside, weep incoherent words
that choke. Mom says *emotions must be stuck
in their throats like broken egg shells.*

R. Nikolas Macioci

A nurse calls my name. I unbend, follow
to a cubicle. Eyes brim tears I hold
back. She notices my somber face, says
a tragic and very sad thing just happened.
I feel lucky but embarrassed I have only
an arm burn, not a life-threatening wound.
We both seem empty of more conversation.
She cleans, rinses, bandages my arm,
releases me, wishes a good rest of the day.

As we amble to the car, I visualize
an unknown street with a burnt-out house,
a street where one less child lives.

DEATH CURE

Waiting for the inevitable exit
from life, our asses black and blue
from that very life, we continue to fall
for propaganda of healing,
use home remedies old as onion poultice
wrapped in wool rags. Even with science
catching on to almost everything,
we still wallow in illnesses.

In the meantime, we learn, because of
PVC hospital tubing, to harbor
an irresistible urge to last as long as we can,
to reach for another glass of water.

We consist of kinetic sparks, essential
electricity that sustains the simple act
of breathing. Over and over,
attempts fail to eliminate death, to strike it
down in its hour, our skins dropping
to the floor with a medicinal glow.
Death breaks our bodies into little pieces,
writes on a tag around the toe
that we cannot as yet laugh at eternal sleep.

R. Nikolas Macioci

PART FIVE

"Sexuality is the lyricism of the masses."

Charles Baudelaire

R. Nikolas Macioci

THE SKIN ACT

He lowers her to the bed. Her lover,
silent, listens to her breathing which
seems to stop until her back rests,
like a floating dogwood blossom,
on taut sheets. Her bones form
around his body, his mouth full of her
anticipation. Streetlight, white as stars,
streams through the hotel window.
Rain slams the casement, gushes down
glass like a transparent intruder.
He whispers tenderness, same words
over and over, uptake of their emotions
strong as rivers. They hover in hazy
bliss, a little crazy from feeling
extraordinary. Sealed in warmth
away from the rest of the world,
they ascend toward satisfaction.
She whimpers, grunts, moans, screams
into the grind of his eyes. Their lips
gulp constant kisses, bodies rise and fall
with fulfillment, reach the peak, collapse,
satin sledgehammers pounding in their skulls.

WHAT HAPPENED AT THE CHATEAU

I slip upon your moonlit bed
and once against you, invent love.
Your beautiful grin emerges from a shadow.
We are making a small history tonight
as we fling our clothes to the floor like cloth
promises. Dressed in the light sheen of summer
sweat, we drift together. Crickets mutter
through the open window, and night is dusted
with stars. We are intentionally mute,
marking each other with delicacy
of small strokes. We own the grace of
each other's kisses. Leaning into the circle
of one another's arms, we quietly entreat
our hearts to a steady rhythm. Your eyes shine
like tears in the dark, anticipate seconds
when I draw you into myself,
and your palpable need disappears
like a magic trick.

Afterwards, we lie together
in comfort of each other's embrace, night
surrounding us with mindless silence, and
we sleep as if to celebrate skin.

THE GIRL WHO PAID TO HAVE A MAN'S ARMS AROUND HER

Avery counts five hundred cash,
places it in an envelope, lays
the envelope on the kitchen counter.
She opens the door after three knocks,
finds Caleb's open-faced smile satisfying.
Welcoming him in, telling him to make
himself comfortable, she excuses herself
to the restroom. He strolls to the kitchen
counter, opens envelope, counts the money.
She returns, leads him to the bedroom
where they both undress.

The room is dark except for scant streetlight
from a window that discloses his brown hair,
green eyes. His six-foot-two frame reveals
abundant time spent at the gym. They slide
onto the bed, embrace. She runs her hands
slowly down his back while he kisses her
breasts. Their love making is a paid-for
prayer, a theology of the flesh. Following
hedonistic pleasure, they loll in
devout silence.

Both balance back into their clothes.
She saunters to a bedside stand, retrieves
an envelope containing a hundred-dollar tip.
At the door, they agree to meet again
whenever her husband is out of town.

R. Nikolas Macioci

SLEEPING WITH A NAZI

He flops onto the bed beside his lover.
She turns to accommodate him. The sheen
of street light anoints her back, the contour
of her buttocks, her crotch luminous as an eye.
She looks into his blank face. Its emptiness
frightens her. His fatigue crests. His limbs
sprawl. This could be an underworld scene
from Chicago, 1925: rampant
criminal is calmed by kept girl, but
this is Germany where gas ovens
prevail over gin bottles and whiskey stills.

He begins to doze. She rides him awake,
wide open, deep in. He chastises her
for hovering like a whore, impaled
on her own satisfaction. His nerves wiggle
like minnows from feet to fingertips.
He rolls over, resumes sleep, the skin
on his back a broad darkness. She risks
resting against the hollow formed by
the valley of his spine. Her breasts,
unaccommodated, brush his flesh with hope.
Like a thief, she wraps an arm around him,
steals a cold caress. She watches
his shallow breathing, slides her hand over
his, heat transferred to her forgotten body.
Turning away, she lies on her back, stares
at the ceiling, assumes he dreams and in them
cannot wait to kill.

WEDDING AT THE HARTSTONE INN, CAMDEN, MAINE

You carried a Queen Elizabeth Rose,
the "World's Favorite Rose," said the cashier
at the farmers market along Route 1.
You wanted only one, said its beauty
was enough. You held the rose for the next
ten miles, sniffing its fragrance until
we reached the inn.

The desk attendant greeted us. We signed
our separate names, and he smirked as if
to say he disapproved of people who slept
together not bound by permanent vows.
Behind us, above our heads, a television
flickered an evangelist's condemnations.

The lobby displayed luxury unlike
the motel we stayed in halfway through
our journey where threadbare carpet emitted
musty odor, and upholstery on sagging couches
lay open like broken milkweed pods.

We hauled luggage to the second floor.
Our room afforded a panoramic view of Camden
Harbor and dozens of sailboats anchored
on sparkling blue water. The room evinced
comfort and the possibility of tenderness.

Deep inside the room, I pulled you against myself,
the kiss holding us together in one spot
as if we wore lead shoes. We lay across illumination
from the harbor, a bed on which we had wings
lifting us from the world, our sweat slick
with starlight. Night, a preacher, performed
the ceremony. The rose lay on a bedside table,
petals grown fragile as intimacy.

UNCERTAIN TENDERNESS

Your skin appears as I have envisioned,
smooth as a spoon, slightly skimmed in sweat,
each drop a miniature flower. Light from
afternoon sun traces your nakedness
makes you look foreign, mystifying,
made up of a history of someone else's touches.
Though obsessed, I don't move against you,
but ask a question to answer your blank stare:
Should we as friends become lovers?

You lie on the bed, ready, sunlight tinting
you the color of cantaloupe. I wish to consummate
this part of your life, and though you have
invited me in, I lie immobile because you are more
of a companion since childhood than a woman
who would open to my hammer of desire.

These last-minute reservations make me
reluctant to let you give me yourself
like gold for safekeeping. You coaxed me
to your bedroom as carefully as you would a bird
and supposed I wouldn't want more justification
than your lust and immoral laughter.

I will dress and leave, tortured by imagination
that is not natural to the expression of love.
Lying on the bed, propped on an elbow,
you look dark and sour as if you wanted me
to apologize for my presence, bolt from bed,
and through the door, as if you still wanted
to be dreamed about afterwards.

R. Nikolas Macioci

THE APPRENTICE'S SELF-PORTRAIT

His mentor stands aside, stolid as ice,
patient, waiting for the next brush stroke.
The boy dabs detail, angles his head
to assess perspective. In his mind,
paint is luminous as words that would roll
from his tongue and sing in a voice
not yet a man's. The easel stands
at the side of the room near a window
where July sun is at its brightest.
The boy is unsure of his next move
because the mentor has taught him
empty spaces and silences count.
The mentor steps toward the painting,
shadows a touch on the boy's shoulder.
The boy turns a hesitant smile toward
the older man. The finished painting
is a near perfect representation
of the boy's seventeen-year-old face,
handsome as Antinous, and, like Hadrian,
the boy is the mentor's weakness.

Drunk on Angel Breath

They share an embrace of attitudes,
agree on the painting's success.
To celebrate the end of an apprenticeship,
the mentor brings out a bottle of Lambrusco.
Even though the boy has not reached drinking age,
the occasion warrants a social violation,
and so the wine is poured, wets each of their lips
like a surrogate kiss.

R. Nikolas Macioci

THE EASE WITH WHICH YOU DEAL WITH DANGEROUS BOYS

You know all about the bar-crowd's machinations,
can spot hearts empty of everything but lust.
It took fifty years of Jack and Cokes to hone
sensitivity to phony, apocryphal people. Yet,
in old age, you still make an occasional stop
at the Holy Bird Bar, hoping for the indefinable
moment when you will meet someone untattered
by the razor cuts of life, someone who can sit
at the bar and ignore the mirror behind liquor bottles.

Tonight, you chance fate again, settle
on a wooden stool and wait for your drink.
Behind you, a quasi disc jockey boosts amps
for Purple Disco Machine's "In the Dark."
On the dance floor, a couple guys attempt moves
beyond their repertoire. They look like spastic
marionettes with someone jerking their strings.
Several more couples hit the floor and appear
less spastic. There's only one empty seat
at the bar, and it remains empty beside you.
You steal peripheral looks either way.
To your left, a clutch of young boys giggle
in near-falsetto shrieks. Four men to your right
stare straight ahead as if stoned
by disenfranchisement and shackled by middle age.
Sometimes, they drop their heads, gaze into their drinks.
They do not talk to each other.

Drunk on Angel Breath

Eventually, the door opens on the man
who will sit beside you. He says hello,
asks if it's okay to buy you a drink.
You're surprised at his interest. You ask his age
and what work he does. He is thirty-six
and not working at the moment. Intuition says
keep your distance. He is handsome and transparent.
You can almost smell his intent as it wafts through
sweet cologne. "Do you have a few bucks I can borrow
until Friday?" You thank him for the drink, slide
from your stool.

As you pass through the crowded patio
and wade into the humid, July night, someone
you don't know yells at your back, "Leaving so soon?"
You start your car and, all of a sudden,
everything outside the claustrophobic bar seems better.

R. Nikolas Macioci

THERE HAS NEVER BEEN A MORE SUCCESSFUL WOMAN

Death, clad in a sparkly, red, spaghetti-strap dress,
shouldering a Prada leather mini bag, and
shod in Jimmy Choo heels, and inevitability,
sachets up and down Figueroa Street in LA.
Soon, a Kia Optima SX pulls to the curb,
passenger window down. He offers to pay
her for time. She looks him over. Paul wears
a navy polo shirt and pasty pallor.
She gets in, and they drive away. He coughs,
and the sound echoes deep and phlegmy.
She's amazed he's lasted this long, but not
surprised he's come to her for a last fling.
They drive to a predetermined destination.
Later, he drops her off where he picked her up,
then steers into inescapable night.
Back on the street, she waits for her next client.
Everyday, all night and day, she continues
this routine to afford expensive clothes, apartment,
a car. Many have begged her to quit, to retire,
but she's stubborn as a fact, and would miss
too much all the people who drive down her street.

UNBEARABLE AND FIERCE MERCY

His sweaty hand slips on the glossy book
cover as he focuses on her standing
behind the cashier's counter. He didn't notice
her when he first entered, but when
he removed a book from the shelf, turned back
toward the entrance, she became his desire.

His hand flips pages without looking.
Her creamy skin, gray eyes, brown hair with
auburn highlights enamor him. He replaces
the book, picks up another, opens it, his
concentration elsewhere. She doesn't notice
him staring at her.

He strolls to another shelf to avoid suspicion,
even though she is still visible. He leans
his head sideways to read titles, finger
skimming one binding after another.
If he were asked, he would admit quick
infatuation smacks of an adolescent crush,

a momentary obsession. He decides
to buy *The Craving Impulse*, a fiction book
with white cover, gold, embossed lettering.
He digs his wallet out, finds his place in line,
wishes he had shaved, prepared for the unforeseen.
Nervous, he motions for the person behind him

to move forward. Minutes later, he's at the checkout,
fumbles out a $20 bill. Except for words to transact
the sale, she says nothing. He slumps out of the shop
to his car, embarrassed by foolish feelings,
steers to the nearest McDonald's, breaks the spell of her
with a burger and fries.

Drunk on Angel Breath

THE NOTHING THAT GROWS INSIDE OF ME

I've loitered in Schiller Park many times
to watch couples walk dogs. How do I
distinguish between myself, who appreciates
seeing happy moments, and a voyeur?
I astound myself with such flagrant attention
to others. I can't understand their language
because they are usually too far away, but
I note their dumb show of emotions:
holding hands, an arm around a shoulder.

Today, I slouch on a bench. Squirrels surround
my sadness, hungry for a handout.
It is mid-March. Nothing much grows yet
except persistent daffodil stems green
as asparagus. I used to think I came here
to meditate, alleviate stress. Now it is plain
I settle for minutes of being
a vicarious part of other people's lives,
ones where I note the apparent
possibility of love.

A couple ambles along a brick sidewalk,
stop to snap pictures of one another.
They take turns standing against the trunk
of a huge oak. After they leave, no evidence
exists they were there except the photograph
which, if I were to see it, would break my heart.

R. Nikolas Macioci

LOVE IN A FIELD OF POPPIES

It's dark. We sit in wicker rockers
on the front porch, silence between us.
You lean your head back and doze,
mouth open like a dead fish.
My suspicions come like worms after a rain,
crawl into consciousness over and over.
I nudge your arm. You awaken,
and, like a hinge on a door, I squeak
out the question. "What drugs
have put wings in your brain, oblivion
on your face." You figit, hesitant to speak,
to open the box with a snake inside.
"Heroin," a weighty word, burns the air.
You take a deep breath, flick a cigarette butt
onto carefully manicured lawn.

I tear from my chair, stride into the house,
rip open cellophane on a pack of peanut
butter crackers, order you into the car.

When I drive you home, your head lulls
against the side window. I drop you
at your house. A sudden hand
of lightning reaches across the sky,
its fingers jagged and white.
As I pull from the curb, thunder grumbles
an echo of something killed in the name of truth.

SAKURA
The Japanese word for cherry blossoms

The lure of a heroin high trumps reason
and restraint. These are words you told me
as you bent out of the car and vomited
into the street. Helpless, I watched puke splash
the curb. Sick from an overdose, you leaned
back in your seat, head drooped, oblivious
of white, cherry blossoms that lined the sidewalk.

April sun flooded the windshield, spread
mellow warmth across the dashboard. We dwelled
silent as two people in a dumb show,
communication out of the question.
I did not want to salvage this tarnished romance.

Sympathy and disgust clashed as I started the car,
headed to your house. We parked in front
of the ramshackled place where you rented a room
when you could afford it. You had an agreement
between the owner and yourself: she would
let you stay there if you bought your heroin from her
and her alone. I hated you both, her for supplying
the drug abyss you'd fallen into and you for being
so susceptible.

I'm sorry you said, turning toward me,
no sign of apology in your green eyes.
I didn't respond. You ducked out of the car.
I sat there for a minute, looked around.
There were no cherry blossoms in this neighborhood.

R. Nikolas Macioci

THINGS I'LL NEVER TOUCH AGAIN

Cassettes, eight-track tapes, VHS video tapes,
35 mm slides, rotary phones, old photographs,
grade cards with failing grades at the bottom
of a cedar chest, out-of-style walking shorts,
pots and pans I never use, books I've already
read, out-of-date cameras, my dad's tools,
bricks stacked at the back of the property,
ladders to climb the roof, a paintbrush, a lawn
mower, a tree trimmer, the banister where I
carved my initials in a New York City hotel,
automobiles that I once owned, logs for the
unused fireplace, a ring of unidentifiable keys,
doorknobs on all the houses I've lived in,
any kind of meat, guacamole, hair dye, the topics
of politics or religion, reference books
Google has replaced, manuals about how to play
various sports, a snow shovel, the piano, pets,
my smooth body before puberty, lives
of those who have died, friends separated
from me by time, place, and interests,
lovers who have drifted into oblivion,
you lying in my bed with your back toward me,
an incomplete tattoo on your arm that stops
near your wrist like an unfinished story.

CAREFUL RETURN

The knock on my door is the sound of you
coming back. We stare at each other.
You ask if you may come in. I step aside,
tell you to have a seat. You fold down
onto the couch. I slump in a club chair
across from you, see the room through your eyes:
a predominantly maroon oriental rug,
a mantle clock, an antique table, another
club chair, a Yorkshire Terrier licking
a stray shoe, cleaning a shadow with its tongue.

I do not tell you to unbutton your peacoat
and stay. In fact, I grit my teeth remembering
how you abandoned me and the world
for the benumbing buzz of heroin.

You drag a cigarette from a pocket, ask
if it's okay? I don't answer because I know
you remember how much I hated
your chain smoking. You light the cigarette.
A deluge of silence floods between us.
I want to scoot forward in my chair and speak,
but my lips are parched, words stuck in my throat
like wet paper wads. I mumble *why didn't you stay
away? You seemed so far off, and that was good.
I've healed, but now you want to rip the scab
from the wound.* You fidget, ask for an ashtray.
I simply glare. You crush the butt in your pocket.

R. Nikolas Macioci

The mantle clock chimes ten times as if
to dismiss this meeting. You rise, take a step
toward me, stop, turn to the door. I don't speak.
In my mind I scribble goodbye to you and
to the kind of love we once knew by heart.

SINGING THE SONG OF WANTING SOMETHING OUT OF REACH

The waiter bends close to bring the check, his
profile toward me. I feel old age
buzz through my body like a surge of blood.
He stands at the table only seconds,
time enough to see eyelashes against
perfect skin, a wisp of beard.
I long for his youth, feel myself crumble
with age. I drum fingers on the table,
anticipate his return with my receipt.
I see my reflection in my cell phone,
tired eyes and slack mouth. Suddenly,
he slips the receipt onto the table,
says thank you, and leaves. Outside, unable
to expel envy, I unlock the car, slide in
embarrassed to have extolled the impossible,
to have let the dull knife of imagination
cut reason to ribbons.

R. Nikolas Macioci

PART SIX

"A day without laughter is a day wasted."

Charlie Chaplin

"Science fiction is filled with Martians and space travel to other planets, and things like that."

Margaret Atwood

R. Nikolas Macioci

GOURMET HOSPITAL FOOD

Only a hospital could ruin a banana.
The straw that came with apple juice
was the best part of breakfast. Oatmeal,
without sugar, lodged on my palate,
a combination of dried grass and mush.
Vegetable broth with too much salt
exceeded my heart-healthy diet.
When I uncapped the fruit cup, I anticipated
a variety of flavors. I tasted
a uniform distaste of wet cardboard.

With defeatist attitude, I greeted
a kitchen worker who leaned against the door
of my room and read the lunch menu.
She started with tuna salad, and I tuna-ed her out.
I could imagine a mixture sopping
with mayonnaise, so I took the high road,
ordered tomato soup and the infamous fruit cup.

Unwilling to risk dinner, I headed
kitchen staff off at the pass, ordered
a pack of peanut butter crackers and Jell-o.
Not the healthiest cuisine, but it was either that
or call the kitchen worker back to my room
and eat the menu itself.

EUCHRE

No one who has tried has successfully
taught me to play euchre. Family, friends,
and even strangers have attempted,
but they all threw up their hands in defeat
or maybe to ask heaven for a reprieve.
The rules, and even the vocabulary,
confuse me. I feel as if I'm trying to learn
to play bridge in twenty minutes. The word
itself would take me down in a spelling bee.
Why isn't it spelled *y-o-u-k-e-r* or *u-k-e-r*?
Even *u-c-e*-r or *u-c-i*-r would make more sense.

Another confusing moment occurs
when I'm supposed to say the word *pass*
which I think is meant to foreworn players
I'm about to relieve myself of gas. Then,
there is the word *trump*, the sound a horse makes,
or is that *tromp*? And whoever heard of
a card game in which aces are relegated
to third place, and jacks are the highest
cards in the pack? Furthermore, most
of the cards are kept in the box. What a waste!
Dare I say players of this game aren't playing
with a full deck? What's more, if someone
orders me up, am I supposed to leave the game?

Drunk on Angel Breath

Then we come to bars which, when I looked
it up, are actually called bowers. There is the left
and right, something like turn signals
in a car, but not as easy to learn. Bars are
the game's prostitutes. They take tricks.
What about skunked? At least there is no smell
until you lose, and that stinks. Nevertheless,
the only bar I understand is the one that serves beer
and liquor, and I'm headed there now to help me
forget everything I never learned about *e u c h r e*.

R. Nikolas Macioci

BATTLE FOR NAPKINS

I thought gold was a good investment,
but apparently napkins is better. Why,
otherwise, is there such a scarcity?
Are workers pocketing them or stashing
them in their lockers? In better restaurants,
it's usual to receive no more than one
napkin with silverware wrapped in it.
Requesting additional napkins yields
only one or two extras.

Recently, in a Chinese eatery,
I requested more napkins, received two
palm-size squares, not enough to cover
my nose in an unexpected sneeze.
Without a paper shortage, the explanation
looms that napkins have quadrupled
their value on Wall Street.

Now and then, I receive a cloth napkin
and no paper napkins at all. The cloth napkin
is useful when spread across the lap, but
it does not suffice to wipe excess food
from the face. I've threatened to bring my own
napkins from home, but recently, found
a solution.

Drunk on Angel Breath

Before my meal at an upscale
restaurant, I entered the restroom first,
yanked half a dozen paper towels
from the dispenser, carried them to my table,
and began folding them like napkins.
Another customer roamed by, stopped
and asked if it was my first day on the job.
I said yes that I was working for minimum wage
and would greatly appreciate a generous tip.

R. Nikolas Macioci

A GOOD MYSTERY NEVER KILLED ANY BODY

What good is life without fear
or a good mystery novel? You navigate
pages, read about a body in a bathtub,
gunshots that ruin a grand piano, ricochet,
kill the femme fatale. Cozy by the fire,
you peruse until late hours, subjugate
sleep to reach the conclusion.
By morning, you slouch near dwindling
fire, continue to comb sentences for clues.
You keep track of bodies found in closets,
maids who dabble in alchemy.
You imagine detectives examining the corpse
before the coroner zips it into a bag.
One thing for sure, someone's hands are
bloody. You aim to find out whose.
Tension is tighter than a tripwire.
Minimal bathroom breaks leave you wiggling
in your wingback chair, but stubborn patience
finally reveals the guilty culprit. The butler?
You've got to be kidding! How could you
have missed so many hints? Details comes back,
signs that could lead to the killer, but
part of the fun was in being deceived.
It's five in the morning. You're headed to bed,
rub blurry eyes, say to yourself you thought
you knew all along who did it, find out,
at the end, you were completely wrong.

THE DOUBLE EDGE OF OWNING A PARROT

I've never wanted to own a parrot
whose mouth cannot be held accountable
for curse words thrown its way.
People believe parrots speak truth
with potent honesty. Actually,
they are expert eavesdroppers that overhear
hundreds of words each day and remember
the most offensive ones.

Omnivores, parrots eat seeds and insects,
and, as if they had been dipped in pigments
from a Benjamin Moore paint store, wear
flamboyant colors of feathered rainbows.

If the world were ruled by parrots,
life would be a love song. Parrots afford
companionship in nursing homes,
show affection, comfort the lonely.

Parrots can't keep secrets, though.
Their tongues disclose adultery
and double-dealing.

In South America and Australia,
poachers procure parrots for pet shops.
A hyacinth macaw can bring more than $8,000.

The parrot symbolizes affection and friendship.
Despite its unpredictability,
the parrot nestles to your face and says
I love you.

R. Nikolas Macioci

IF BIRDS WERE MONEY

How many swans does it cost for a beer?
A bag of Fritos or chips comes to
a couple of blackbirds. Pull a parrot
from its perch and pay for a pizza.
Three sparrows will buy a theater ticket.
Popcorn is one parakeet, candy, a chickadee.
Grab a continental breakfast for one
bunting and an evening meal for a mallard.
Pay rent with a half-dozen parakeets,
or buy your house outright with a hyacinth
macaw. Secure your future with a scarlet
tanager worth of stock. Cancel your credit-card
debt with a cardinal and open a bank account
worth a dozen bluebirds. Give your love
an engagement band for one ring-necked pheasant.
Pay for the wedding with warblers, and when
you're in an economic pinch, reach for a finch.
You can cover monthly bills with a coot,
canary, or cockatoo. It's wise to accumulate
as many owls as you can for retirement, and
while you're building your nest, you might
want to stash a few storks. In the end,
spend your birds wisely, don't go cuckoo,
or become a profligate with your feathered assets.
Remember, toucan live as cheaply as one.

WASHINGTON CIRCLE

I live in Washington Circle, a small town
south of Columbus, Ohio.
A fountain in the middle of the town square
boasts a bronze statue of George Washington
reared on his horse, the proverbial pose
of conquerors and corrupt politicians.
The circle's fame stems from spurious fact
that, on his way pass the fountain,
George allowed his nag to guzzle feculent water.

The town's residents bring fresh meaning
to the word eccentric. For example, the mayor
writes M-A-R-E before his name,
causing everyone to speculate
if it's because he's often been called
a horse's ass.

Beulah Lightumup's son says she was born
with a cigarette in her mouth, so,
for her last birthday, he fashioned
a necklace of butts to ridicule her
for compulsive chain smoking.

Now turn to Mary Louise Randy,
Randy being the name of Rachel
Randy's dog that follows Mary Louise
close enough for neighbors to wonder
which of the two is randy.

Priscilla Paydirt delivers dump trucks
of soil. She also delivers dirt
on everyone in town.

R. Nikolas Macioci

If you plan to visit Washington Circle,
though the town doesn't brag about
a fountain of youth, you can depend
on a taste of stagnant water from the pool
in which GW's horse perpetually gallops.

THREE HOURS FROM ATHENS, GREECE, 1970

I disembark the ship from Italy,
stand for a moment on a winding,
rural road leading to the bus
that will take me to Athens.
A man materializes from nowhere.
His trousers bag, shirt, sweat-soaked,
loss of teeth apparent when he smiles.
He grabs my luggage, starts trudging
down the hot, dirt road. Shouting
what is he doing elicits a babbled
explanation I don't understand.
I race after him as fast as I can.
He is disappearing. My suitcases bang
against his thighs like saddlebags. Wait,
I yell, face burning from sun, dust spiraling
upward from footsteps.

I catch up, grip his shoulder, he stops,
bewildered. His brown eyes reveal
no understanding. I seize my bags. He glowers,
confused. I do not know Greek,
cannot tell him why I must carry stuff
in an opposite direction before I miss my ride.

I dig in my pocket, hand him an unknown quantity
of drachma. He looks even more perplexed.
I lift suitcases away from his frustration,
away from him trying to make a meager living,
a man whose mind, I imagine, reaches for a reason
I paid him to be empty-handed.

PHANTASMAGORIC MIGRATION

I praise the injured sweep of broken birds,
watch them ruined by winter. Do they ponder
God the way I do or simply go with echoing
wings to where they stumble onto stray warmth?
Somedays, reveries seem to color sky
bluer than blue, and birds slip from shadows
of their own lives into sovereign clouds
that have the same exact look as death.
I found myself talking to those fragile birds
just before they faded over and over into
the chocking heat of Brazil. The roof
of my mind remembers the downy heads
of those birds, their crazy eyes turning back
to fasten a final look on me.

Now, I am as alone as a snake's rattle,
and the best birds have cleared out of town,
clogged air with escape. Now that they
are as gone as an old mill, I resent
my urge to be rid of them. They've left
the dying ones behind to talk to themselves,
to bear with ease their wrecked lives.

Was it my roving imagination that loved
those birds, that strummed the wires
on which they waited for handfuls of sacred
bread? We were made to part when time
sung out the end, but daily I lust for the
feathery sound of their unfailing return.

ESCAPADE

"For 19 years I lived in metropolitan Baltimore,
and whenever a snowstorm approached, people
would hoard toilet paper, and I never understood why?"

Jo Jo Girard

Coming from separate aisles
in Dollar General, both women spy
a twelve-pack of toilet paper,
on an otherwise empty shelf.
The women fly to the item,
reach the shelf, grab the package,
pull it in opposite directions.
Plastic splits, and paper hits the floor.
One roll unwinds like giant gauze.
Toilet tissue aside, the ladies clutch
each other until they are closer
than two halves of a walnut shell.
They grapple onto the ground. One
snatches a box of cookies from atop
a huge bag of dog chow from the other
woman's cart. Cellophane breaks,
and cookies roll like chocolate wheels.
The women wrestle as if survival were the prize.

Loud profanity brings the manager swooping
into sight. He kneels down, pries them apart.
When everyone is standing again,
one of the women winds toilet paper back
onto a cardboard cylinder. The manager divides
the spoils between the women, tells them to pay,
leave the store, and not come back.
Angry, exasperated, they exit
down the same aisle, snarl at each other
loud enough to be heard across the store.
The lady yells at the woman with dog chow,
"I hope your dog gets poison ivy on its ass,
and you too."

GAS STATION BLUES

The sign says $3.22 per gallon.
I whip into the station, park
in front of the regular pump. Another glance
and the sign reads $3.50 per gallon.
I turn off the ignition, jump from the car,
insert my debit card into the gas-pump slot.
Another glimpse of the sign reveals per-gallon
price hiked to $4. I'm frantic to fill my tank
before the price hits $5.

While I'm pumping liquid gold into my tank,
I notice my rear tire on the driver's side
is flatter than a snake's belly. Finished
depleting my bank account, I steer
to the air pump. It costs $2, coins only,
for three minutes. I don't have change.
I go to the booth and ask the cashier
to give me $5 worth of quarters. A little
extra never hurt. She looks at me
as if I had asked her to pawn her wedding ring.
I fill my pockets with coins, return
to the air machine.

Drunk on Angel Breath

I insert eight quarters. The hose wiggles
like a strand of Medusa's hair. I stretch
the tubing to fill the driver's side first, but
the line is about a foot too short.
I restart the car, maneuver closer to the pump.
This time the hose reaches, but the pump has quit.
Eight more quarters, and I'm in business again.
It takes every coin I have to fill all four tires.
I'm exhausted, need some air myself, worry
someone overheard my thoughts and will start
charging for breath.

Back in the car, happy to see the gauge needle
on full, bone-weary, dog-tired from absurdities,
I lean forward with determination,
set the GPS destination to the nearest dealership
for electric cars.

ZOOMING

I have yet to attend a zoom meeting
in more than my shirt and boxers.
After all, who can see under the table
or desk? If it weren't so conspicuous
I would take off my shirt, too. At least,
so far, I haven't tried to stand up
and do the Macarena or been arrested
for indecent exposure. It's not that I'm
so immodest. It's just more comfortable
to be as unclad as possible. I worry
about days when we will go back to
in-person conferencing. Dare I say
I will be tempted to attend in my skivvies.
The difference between shorts and a pair
of boxers is a matter of an inch or two
more cloth. Also, how do I know
what's going on under other people's tables
or desks? Maybe they're doing a Lady
Godiva while I am more clad than Tarzan.
If anyone ever discovers my attire, or lack
of it, they have been in the wrong place
at the wrong time. What's the point of clothes
anyway? People always wonder what's under
them. Why not satisfy their curiosity
and resolve the question once and for all?
In conclusion, all I can say is at my computer,
nudity is looming while I am zooming.

TIME ON THE MOON

It's a measure of skill to walk on rocks.
You ask where is everyone else? They're shining
down on you from behind Earth's picket fence.
They're looking at your light through their dining
room window. You can go naked now, if you want.
No one will see you in Times Square or Seattle.
Do you concede that a view of the Earth
from here is breathtaking?

Build a house with a floor and a roof. Bathe
the windows in stars. Mail postcards regularly
to those who think the moon is only a story.
These are the best times you will ever have.
Your head should swell with privilege. If you cry
for home, remember, you turned away from it
once, glad to be in a different place.

You're standing on the moon that used to shine
into your bedroom on God only knows how
many lonely nights. You never did pull
the drapes shut. That's the craziest thing to do,
letting it infiltrate your heart with a hunger
for romance. You survived in your room
glutted with light, and now here you are walking
on the source.

You will not cry anymore. That is
an advantage to this place. Tears do not fall.
They become remembrances. Unlike on Earth,
you will dwell under a soundless sky with nobody
to rob you of your sadness.

R. Nikolas Macioci

ASSET FROM ANOTHER WORLD

A star sticks to the nape of his neck
like an interplanetary kiss. His first
day in Farmersville, suspicion rises
like hair on a cat's back. Folks do not
notice transparent, green eyes or
the odor of outer space he emits, but
talk of the star spreads fast as a missile.
Drunks at The Mahogany Bar want
to aim guns at the stranger who entered
town as if on a wisp of cosmic magic.
Neighbors gawk from windows, wait
to glimpse the man with the star
who ambles up the walk to Mrs. Beringer's
bed and breakfast. He asks to rent
a room of dreams which startles her
into believing him crazy dangerous.
Her body tenses when he utters
language she doesn't recognize,
words that mean he offers love
and peace. She grabs her phone, pokes
the sheriff's number, says she's afraid
of the man who stands in her foyer.
Minutes later, sheriff and deputy skid
to a stop, rush steps to her door.
Neither sheriff nor deputy learn
where the man came from, want to push
him to the rim of the earth or back
to wherever he originated.
The alien writes the word "harmony"
in dust on the entryway table.
The law cuffs him, leads him to the cruiser,
pushes his head down under the doorframe.

Drunk on Angel Breath

The police station is only blocks away.
The car brakes at the curb. The sheriff
glances in the rearview mirror, shocked
to see the back seat empty.

R. Nikolas Macioci

PART SEVEN

"A poet is, before anything else, a person who is passionately in love with language."

W.H. Auden

R. Nikolas Macioci

NO WORDS

There are no words in this poem. Imagine
you are looking at a white, wentletrap,
seashell you found this morning several
inches from the Atlantic. Sun, a fist of fire,
spread silver fingers across waves crumbling
to shore, smoothed a palm of light over sand,
but no words washed shoreward. A kind of
seeing did and permeates you brain with
pictures like a second sight. You watch
a gull scream out of the sky, half bird,
half hymn. So far, no words have washed in
on whitecaps either. I am right there with you,
wanting to see what follows the chill of no
language. Look up. Attach to sky and clouds
the inside color of an oyster shell. Does it
seem you loiter on the lip of the world, waiting
for verbal variables to beach like rare driftwood?
The ocean is a deep mirror. Look into it. Witness
elegant fluctuation of shadowy fish. Feel sensual
flourish of centuries-old breezes fan your flesh, all
without language. Wade through seagrass,
rouse the spice of feeling, yellow-green whispers
brushing your ankles. The moment is personal
as breath, and you can't nor want to name it
because you have no names. Nothing
approximates an amble along coastline when
sunset washes everything in finality, yellowish-red
of Hell hovering at the horizon. No marks on
paper can conjure that ancient sight. Letters
stumble. Sentences deceive. I have given you
sun, sea, grass without pen or pencil. You did not
see me scribble these things on a pad. It was
sort of a dance between experience and deception.

R. Nikolas Macioci

You have seen spume off whitecapped waves,
night crawling into place like a black spider,
futility of a useless grip on the urgency
of words. Leave your legal pad empty.
A blank page delivers the highest level
of meaning.

SKY'S WHORE

I lull at my desk, soft flesh of triceps
sagging, bifocals polished to a shine.
To please editors, I must remove
the poets' sin, moon, from my writing,
ignore it's pull, it's lure to go outside
at midnight and hobble down a garden
walk of mossy stones. It's brilliance,
like white blood, slants into my office,
brightens a blank page. It's luminescence
seems to beg for trivia and nonsense.

I avoid being transfixed, drag myself
away from its appeal, want to write
a clean, well-crafted poem without
celestial interference. Ambling
to the window, I take one last look,
pull the blind. Pen in hand, I
steer clear of romantic inclinations,
scribble *let me alone, cancel seduction,
take your clichés elsewhere.*

THE POET WANTS MORE THAN POETRY

His greed for alcohol equals his avarice
for words. In a sleazy part of town,
he slumps at a desk in a rented room,
hungry, not for food but for poems.
He compresses the English language
into obscure verse so tight it suggests
insanity.

He leans over his desk, idle
as sun, waits for an idea to flood
his mind. He considers writing
about the sea, riddles the poem with gulls
and indecipherable images.

He slaves for sound, cherishes words
that would yield everlasting music,
words more perfect then the works
of a watch.

He crumples another poem,
pitches it into the waste basket,
plods to the kitchen, mixes a scotch
and soda cocktail.

Drunk on Angel Breath

Back at the desk, the idea of night
catches fire. He begins to write
about shadowy people outside
his window who loiter on the street
for quick sex. From dirty-curtained
casement, he has seen such people
lean empty lives through car windows,
frame a deal to fulfill desire. He scribbles
the body can't say no to possibility
of its own satisfaction.

He finishes the poem and another scotch
and soda, stretches out on a single bed,
turns on his side, thinks of hours
of Johnnie Walker it took to drag a poem
from himself.

R. Nikolas Macioci

MORE UPBEAT POEMS PLEASE

My good friend wants to know why
I don't write more positive poems.
Unlike her, who had an almost perfect
childhood, I hung upside down in Hades
during mine. Incidents abound:
There's the one about my dad locking me
in the coalbin on New Year's Eve.
I can still hear the lock click shut,
trapping me in darkness. Another
moment haunts when Dad, roaring
drunk, fell into our Christmas tree
and destroyed Mom's meticulous
decorating. Voluminous stories
tumble like poison fruit from despair's
cornucopia. At the core of each
account is something ugly, something
burnt around the edges with brutality.
As a child, heart tangled with conflict,
I felt caged in the middle of my parents'
combustible moments, cornered, choking
on the smoke of their incendiary
relationship. So, I tell the stories I can
while the burning goes on into adulthood
because it never rains in Hell.

About the Author

R. Nikolas Macioci earned a PhD from The Ohio State University, and for thirty years taught for the Columbus City Schools. In addition to English, he taught Drama and developed a Writers Seminar for select students. OCTELA, the Ohio Council of Teachers of English, named Nik Macioci the best secondary English teacher in the state of Ohio.

Nik is the author of two chapbooks:
- Cafes of Childhood and Greatest Hits

as well as seventeen other books:
- Why Dance?
- Necessary Windows
- Cafes of Childhood (original with additional poems)
- Mother Goosed
- Occasional Heaven
- A Human Saloon
- Rustle Rustle Thump Thump
- Rough
- The Melancholy Life of Doris Menning
- Stoney Seasons
- A Feast of Losses
- Gods of Disharmony
- The Only Country I've Been Dead In
- Dark Guitar
- City of Hammers
- The Hot Ice Cream Empire
- Another Chance in Eden

Critics and judges called *Cafes of Childhood* a "beautifully harrowing account of child abuse," but not "sentimental" or "self-pitying," an "amazing book," and "a single unified whole." *Cafes of Childhood* was submitted for the Pulitzer Prize in 1992. In addition, more than two hundred of his poems have been published here and abroad in magazines and journals, including *Chiron Review, Concho River Review, The Bombay Review,*

The Raven's Perch, The Main Street Rag, and *West Trade Review*

He won First Place in the 1987 National Writers' Union Poetry Competition, judged by Denise Levertov, First Place in The Baudelaire Award Competition, sponsored by The World Order of Narrative and Formalist Poets (1989), Second Place in *Zone 3*'s first annual Rainmaker Awards, judged by Howard Nemerov (1989), and Second Place in the *Writer's Digest* annual competition, judged by Diane Wakoski (1991). In 2021, he was nominated for a Pushcart Prize and a Best of the Net award. In 2022, he was nominated for a Pushcart Prize. He was nominated for a Best of the Net award for 2023, and again for the Pulitzer Prize in 2024 for his book *City of Hammers*.